Unspoken Grief

Unspoken Grief

Coping with Childhood Sibling Loss

Helen Rosen
Rutgers
The State University of New Jersey

Lexington Books
D.C. Heath and Company/Lexington, Massachusetts/Toronto

Library of Congress Cataloging in Publication Data
Rosen, Helen.
   Unspoken grief.

   Bibliography: p.
   Includes index.
   1. Death—Psychological aspects—United States. 2. Death—Social aspects—United States.
3. Brothers and sisters—United States. 4. Bereavement—Psychological aspects. I. Title.
HQ1073.5.U6R67 1986   155.9'37   85-40389
ISBN 0-669-11024-8 (alk. paper)
ISBN 0-669-11022-1 (pbk. : alk. paper)

Published simultaneously in Canada
Printed in the United States of America
Casebound International Standard Book Number: 0-669-11024-8
Paperbound International Standard Book Number: 0-669-11022-1
Library of Congress Catalog Card Number: 85-40389

The paper used in this publication meets the minimum requirements of American National
Standard for Information Sciences—Permanence of Paper for Printed Library Materials,
ANSI Z39.48-1984.

To Karen, in memoriam

Contents

Tables

Foreword

Richard A. Gardner, M.D.
Columbia University
College of Physicians and Surgeons

I am in agreement with Dr. Helen Rosen that sibling loss has not been given the attention it deserves in the psychological literature. Although more prevalent in previous centuries—when parents had to have twice as many children as they ultimately hoped would survive—childhood sibling loss is still common enough to warrant special investigation. We are indebted to Dr. Helen Rosen for her contribution in this area. Her book provides a wealth of theoretical information, culled from an exhaustive search of the relatively limited available literature. But she does not stop there. She includes findings from her own research and clinical experiences with her patients.

Although the death of a parent is more psychologically traumatic to a child than the death of a sibling, a sibling death is still a formidable stress. I found of particular value Dr. Rosen's discussion of the wide variety of inappropriate parental reactions to a child's death, especially those reactions involving surviving children. Parents deny, avoid discussions, foster conspiracies of silence, lie, and exhibit other inappropriate reactions that interfere with the surviving children's capacity to deal optimally with the sibling loss. Dr. Rosen's descriptions of children's reactions that result from such parental maneuvers provide compelling evidence of the need for parents to be open, honest, and direct with their children regarding sibling loss and for therapists to encourage communication and free expression of feelings among all the bereaved.

The author recalls in this regard seeing a six-year-old child who presented with the chief complaint of severe fears of separation from her mother. Three months prior to my initial consultation her teenage brother had died of leukemia, and it was soon therafter that the symptoms began. Inquiry revealed that the parents had told the patient (their only surviving daughter) almost nothing about the sudden disappearance of her brother. They just said that he had gone to heaven. The family lived primarily in a foreign country and was temporarily living in the United States in association with the father's business obligations. At the time of the brother's death the parents and child flew back to their native country, with the brother's coffin in the hold of the airplane. The patient was not told that the body of her dead brother was on the plane. When they arrived in their native country, the patient was whisked away to the home of friends, during which time the parents arranged for and attended the brother's funeral services and burial. All of this was withheld from the patient. On return to the United States the patient exhibited the aforementioned symptom. She insisted upon remaining always at her mother's side. She refused to attend school, and she would not visit outside the home. When someone would come to the door, she would flee into her bedroom and hide in the closet or under the bed.

On the basis of my initial evaluation I concluded that the parents' failure to give the patient accurate information about her brother's death was the cause of her symptomatology. From her vantage point, a person could suddenly be removed from the face of the earth without known cause. Perhaps the abduction took place while one was in the street going to school. Perhaps children were taken away while visiting the homes of other children, or perhaps someone would come to the door and take her away to "heaven." Whatever the method and circumstances of removal, the patient reasoned that the best way to protect herself from this catastrophe would be to remain continually at her mother's side.

I encouraged the parents to be direct and honest with the patient about the circumstances concerning her brother's death. Although initially reluctant, they agreed to do so. Within a week there was a complete alleviation of all symptoms. During this time the patient exhibited a normal mourning reaction, which included repeatedly questioning her parents about the details of her brother's death. This case demonstrates some of the main points emphasized so compellingly by Dr. Rosen in *Unspoken Grief.*

This book fills a need that should have been met long ago. Dr. Rosen appreciated well this gap in our knowledge and has risen admirably to the challenge of providing us with important information in this previously neglected area.

Acknowledgments

The research that forms the basis of much of this book received support from the Rutgers University Research Council. I also owe my thanks to the many undergraduate and graduate social work students who helped out in various phases of the study. They include Harriette L. Cohen, Yvonne Kay, Suzanne Smith, Sheila Allen, Barbara Cardile, Barbara Cortese, Judy Frank, Sharon Gwienze, George Hayman, Barbara Heinhold, Cynthia Hesser, Retha Hughes, Rosemary Hughes, Diahnne Johnson, Ella Loebell, Nancy Maldonado, Emma McElliott, Rita Nowak, Nancy Roberts, Racein Siler, Lorraine Smail, Jennifer Turner, Kathy Young, Robert Hirsch, and Janine Mariscotti. My thanks to Milton H. Donaldson, M.D., Debbie Feierman, M.S.W., and Judy Strassman, B.A., at Cooper Hospital/University Medical Center in Camden, New Jersey, and to Kathleen Stowell and Ray Gibson from Winslow Township, New Jersey.

My very special thanks to Dr. Richard Gardner for reviewing the manuscript, and to Braulio Montalvo, who gave generously of his ideas and enthusiasm; and especially to Brenda Jackson, for her excellent typing; and to my parents, for their patience, love, and support.

I owe a special debt of gratitude to my husband, whose indefatigable belief in the value of my work sustained me, and to my daughter, Nora, whose patience far exceeded that of most three-year-olds!

Last, and most important, my thanks to the individuals and families that talked with me about their loss and grief. Their wish and mine is that others will benefit from the experiences they so generously shared with me.

Unspoken Grief

1
Introduction

There is no death more difficult to endure than the death of a child. The death of a child moves us all, stimulating our deepest sense of injustice and empathy. While never easy to accept, death in old age makes some sense to us and at least provides the satisfaction of a full life span. We revolt against the idea of a life unable to fulfill its potential and against the thought of parents outliving their offspring. We recoil from the failure to nurture and protect a being who from the beginning elicits our strongest feelings of nurturance and protection. The death of a child makes us all feel vulnerable. Yet, approximately 3.5 million children (aged nineteen or under) die each year.[1] And while the overall death rate for Americans has been dropping (by 20 percent from 1960 to 1978), for young people fifteen to twenty-four years old it has actually grown (by 11 percent during the same time period),[2] ensuring that many of us will be touched more or less directly by this tragic event sometime in our lives.

A child's death affects many individuals, both relatives and those outside the family arena. There are shocked and grieving parents and grandparents, relatives of the extended family, schoolmates and friends, even teachers and neighbors who feel the impact of the loss. Often there are siblings of the child who has died. Usually the siblings are children themselves who, in their varying stages of maturation and development, must cope with an event for which they are often totally unprepared.

Although we know and can appreciate a good deal concerning the impact of death on adults, we are far less knowledgeable about the impact of death on children. Because children are unable to express themselves as directly and fluently as adults can, there is still much mystery surrounding their inner life. It is difficult, if not impossible, for us fully to understand the meaning a child attaches to any death. And while we would expect a child in some ways to respond to the death of a brother or sister as he or she would to the death of any significant family member, in other ways, a child's response to the death of a sibling is unique. Only siblings share the same parents and grow up in the same household. In old age, siblings may be our only remaining family.

For many of us, our relationships with our brothers and sisters will be the most extended ones of our lives. When a child experiences the death of a sibling, he loses someone who has been a unique participant in his life, someone who has fulfilled a role that no other person can.

The impact of that death on the child and on the family to which the child belongs is the subject of this book. While we cannot hope to have uncovered the full meaning of this event, there is much that we have discovered that sheds light on it. But before we look specifically at sibling loss, we must consider what we know about childhood bereavement in general—how children cope with the loss of a parent, whether children can be said to grieve and mourn, and the meaning of death to children. These issues form a foundation upon which we will build our understanding of childhood sibling loss.

Children's Reactions to the Death of a Parent

When a child's mother or father dies, a wide range of both normal and pathological reactions is possible. It is an event of unparalleled importance, of potentially lifelong significance.

A child whose parent has died may "view the parent's death to be an abandonment and may fear that the remaining parent will either die or abandon [him] as well."[3] He or she may evidence grief and anger, denial, hopelessness, intellectual problems, guilt, phobic reactions, regression, depression, insomnia, eating disturbances, loss of trust, separation anxiety, and idealization of the dead parent.[4] Early parental death has been associated tentatively with behavior disorders in later life[5] and with predisposition to adolescent suicide.[6] H. Nagera views the death of a parent as a developmental interference. In the event of parental loss, he writes,

> The child is forced to carry on with his psychological development in the absence of one essential figure. This frequently leads to distortions of development and at least tends to complicate the resolution of many of the otherwise normal and typical developmental conflicts of childhood and adolescence. In this way the ground is prepared for a variety of neurotic conflicts that take, as their point of departure, the inappropriate resolution of such developmental conflicts.[7]

Developmental interference of this kind will vary in nature, depending on the phase of development the child is in, and will occur independently of the other meanings attached to the event, for example, a child's belief that he or she caused the death.

Mourning in Childhood

A prominent theme that arises with regard to parental loss is the question of children's capacity to mourn. Beginning with Freud's classic exposition of grief work in "Mourning and Melancholia" and continuing through most of the literature on adult bereavement, the ability to express grief and sorrow following the loss of a loved one has been associated with coping and adaptation.[8] According to Peretz, "If the lost loved or valued object was emotionally significant in the life of the bereaved, the absence of a grief reaction or symptoms of bereavement suggests a prognosis of future maladaptation."[9] With children, however, the situation is much less clear. Observation of bereaved children has led to contradictory conclusions. Speculations range from John Bowlby's view that infants as young as six months old experience mourning reactions identical to those seen in adults[10] to Wolfenstein's belief that the capacity to mourn is not acquired until adolescence.[11] In between are those that believe the ability to grieve is acquired sometime in childhood, as ego functions mature and/or the ability to comprehend the finality of death is achieved. R. Furman, for example, places the capacity to mourn at around three and one half to four years of age, following the ability to comprehend death at approximately two and one half and increased maturation of the mental apparatus at around three.[12] He acknowledges, however, that certain factors can also inhibit reactions at this age, making it appear as if the child cannot mourn. Anna Freud specified that in order for mourning to be possible, an individual must possess certain ego capacities, among them reality testing, acceptance of the reality principle, and control of id tendencies.[13] These capacities are assumed to be absent in the young child.

It should be pointed out that even the term *mourning* has been used with varying meanings in the literature on parental death. Some psychoanalysts subscribe to a highly specialized meaning—"to accept a fact in the external world (the loss of the cathected object) and to effect corresponding changes in the inner world (withdrawal of libido from the lost object)"[14]—while others use the term to denote a broad spectrum of responses. Both Kliman and Gardner, for example, feel that it can be applied to the totality of responses that occur when a parent dies.[15]

A Child's Comprehension of Death

Further complicating our understanding of childhood bereavement is the question of when a child is capable of comprehending the finality of death and the role such comprehension plays in the mourning process. As already mentioned, R. Furman assigns the ability to comprehend death to approximately two to three years of age. This is far earlier than previous research in this area had indicated, in particular Maria Nagy's classic work. In her study of Hungarian children, Nagy observed three stages in a child's conception of death. In the first stage, from approximately three to five years of age, death is envisioned as a departure, with the dead maintaining existence somewhere else; the finality of death is denied. In the second stage, between the ages of five and nine, death is personified; it exists, but can be avoided (only *some* children die). In the third and final stage, at the age of nine or ten, death is understood to be an inevitable occurrence that happens to all people; it is understood realistically.[16]

More recent observers have found strong evidence indicating that at least for some children, death is realistically understood a good deal earlier than Nagy's work suggests. Spinetta and Deasy-Spinetta observed children between the ages of six and ten who understood the meaning of death.[17] These children were cancer patients, which led the researchers to propose that the experience of living with a life-threatening illness may accelerate the process of comprehending the finality of death. Myra Bluebond-Langner, also working with terminally ill children, found that such children may feel they will alienate people if they talk about death and thus do not always share all they know. This withholding may lead to mistaken beliefs about the child's inability to understand death.[18] Dr. Richard Gardner reports having interviewed a four-year-old child with leukemia who, when asked how old he was, said, "I'm four, but I'm never going to be five."[19]

Many believe that the ability to comprehend the finality of death is essential to grieving, but it should be noted that even on this point there is no unanimity of opinion. Schell and Loder-McGough suggest that it is not necessary for a child to have a realistic concept of death in order to grieve. They propose that in any case the child will react to the separation and that "after all, . . . the main thing to which we all react emotionally in a grief situation is the separation itself."[20] Finally, it is important to note that comprehension of the finality of death may come in two stages. First, an appreciation that others can die develops, and later, a recognition that the child himself can die is achieved. Stage one may precede stage two by as much as a few years, evincing a phenomenon that underscores the strength of the child's ability to use denial.[21]

Childhood Sibling Loss

Children's reactions to the loss of a sibling, as opposed to the loss of a parent, have received much less attention from researchers and writers interested in childhood bereavement. This is due in part to our belief that sibling relationships are secondary and relatively unimportant when compared to parent/ child relationships. As Bank and Kahn suggest:

> We had been taught that siblings are, at best, minor actors on the stage of human development, that their influence is supposed to be fleeting, and that it is the parents who principally determine one's identity. . . . The prevailing theories of human development seemed strangely silent about siblings.[22]

In addition, the psychoanalytic emphasis on sibling rivalry as the only remarkable dimension of sibling relationships and the complex methodological issues involved in sibling research have served to discourage extensive projects in this area.[23] Some of the early research in sibling death did raise issues of potential impact of the loss, including a connection between sibling loss and schizophrenia,[24] depression, anxiety, guilt, psychosomatic disorders, and behavior problems.[25] Lauretta Bender's observation showed that children react to the death of the sibling "with all the psychological mechanisms that are common in grief and mourning in the adult."[26] Other studies indicated that while sibling loss does not necessarily result in severe pathology, a wide range of disturbed reactions is possible.[27] These include guilt reactions, death phobias, disturbances in cognitive functioning, and distorted concepts of illness, death, doctors, hospitals, and religion. Blinder suggested that reactive disorders in children occur primarily when the bereavement process for the dead child is truncated.[28]

Only occasionally has sibling loss been examined in the context of the family. The death of a child can significantly disrupt the structure and organization of the family, and parental grief and mourning can hinder surviving siblings in their efforts to adapt.[29] This may occur even with the death of an infant, as in SIDS (sudden infant death syndrome).[30]

Krell and Rabkin described three types of survivor children, based on family dynamics and reactions to the loss.[31] They identified the "haunted child," the "bound child," and the "resurrected child." The haunted child is distrustful and fearful because of silence in the family surrounding the circumstances of the sibling's death. The bound child is overprotected as a result of the family's attempt to prevent further catastrophe. The resurrected child is the surviving child or new infant who has become a replacement for the child who died. These are not uncommon reactions to the loss of a child.

Differences between Parental Loss and Sibling Loss in Childhood

Knowledge of the differences between parental loss and sibling loss is essential to an understanding of the bereaved child's experience. First and foremost, it must be recognized that the loss of a sibling does not present the child with the survival issues posed by the loss of a parent (at least, not to the same degree). With parental loss, a child may fear that "he will no longer be provided with food, clothing, shelter, and other necessities of life."[32] In fact, there is the potential for the child to experience significant environmental deprivation following the loss of a parent. Loss of income, a move to a new residence, and changes in child-care arrangements can accompany the loss of a parent and further strain the child's ability to cope. If the primary caretaker has died, it is usually recommended that a substitute be provided as quickly as possible who will reestablish a sense of continuity of care, since loss of a parent may cause a major disruption in the child's world that affects his or her daily life in innumerable ways. This is not generally the case when a sibling dies.

Loss of a parent also entails the "developmental interference" described by Nagera earlier. Ample evidence exists of the need for continuous availability of the parent during the childhood years. Loss of a parent during childhood poses a very serious threat to the child's development, even under the most optimal circumstances.

On the other hand, we know significantly less about the role of siblings in the formation of the personality. Most recently, Bank and Kahn have proposed eight patterns of sibling identification that accompany the most common sibling relationships.[33] At one extreme are "fused" relationships, where siblings lack differentiation from one another, each feeling like an extension of the other's self. At the other extreme are negative and distant relationships, where anger, hostility, and rigid differentiation predominate. In partial identification, there is a positive and flexible sense of sameness *and* difference which allows a "constructive dialectic." Bank and Kahn suggest that when a child dies who was in either of the two extreme forms of sibling relationships, there is greater potential for pathology to develop in the surviving sibling. Braulio Montalvo adds that in some families a deceased sibling's role may have included exclusive "interpersonal right" in fostering a particular attribute or belief about the surviving sibling. When the child dies, the belief about the surviving sibling dies also, as demonstrated by the remark, "She was the only one who thought I was funny."[34] Thus, both the quality of the sibling relationship and the role occupied by the deceased child vis-á-vis the surviving sibling's sense of self may affect the degree to which the loss of a sibling will impact on personality formation.

Finally, in parental loss, a child is generally perceived by those around him to have suffered an important loss. Generally, they recognize the seriousness of the loss and the need to accommodate to the child's needs, and they are sensitive to feelings of loss or grief in the child. Of course, this is not always the case; sensitivity to the child's needs varies, depending on the family and its ability to adapt. In general, though, there is an awareness that the child has experienced a significant loss, and this awareness will be evident in the behavior of others toward the child. With both parental and sibling loss, a child may experience a range of emotions including guilt, anger, grief, and abandonment, and in either situation, the child may attempt to deal with these powerful feelings through denial or suppression; but in the case of sibling loss, the child's experience may be further complicated by the failure of those around him or her even to acknowledge that he or she has suffered a significant loss. The child may be coping not only with the loss of a sibling but also with the functional loss of grieving parents as well. At the same time, he or she may be viewed by others not only as needing less social support than the parents, but even as being capable of providing that social support *to* the parents. The social reality of sibling loss thus differs from parental loss to a very significant degree.

The Social Pathology of Mourning

There is another aspect of childhood bereavement that is of major concern to those who study sibling loss. In both parental and sibling loss—and characterizing our attitudes toward bereavement of all kinds—is a phenomenon which Braulio Montalvo has called the social pathology of mourning.[35] This pathology derives from our tendency to view bereavement as a private and personal experience. In our social relationships, we respect the individual's need for privacy, we hesitate to bring up a discussion of the deceased, and we abide by the belief that one needs to grieve alone. Even a ritual that is intended to provide support to the bereaved, such as the three-to-seven-day Jewish period of mourning called Shivah, may fail to provide it. In contemporary Britain, as Colin Parkes points out,

> while it is true that the Shivah still serves its traditional function of drawing the family together at a time of bereavement, there is a tendency for it to be used as a distraction from grief rather than as an occasion for its expression. Conversation with the bereaved person often takes the form of neutral chat and the expression of overt emotion is avoided, as it is in other, "public" situations. The "successful" mourner is thought to be the one who shows a proper control of his feelings on all occasions. In such circumstances the funeral, wake or Shivah becomes an ordeal which is likely to be viewed with mixed feelings.[36]

Professionals also commonly view the process of mourning as an intrapsychic one. Rarely do they actively acknowledge that mourning is not solely a private matter; that not only does the individual who is mourning live in a family, but he or she also lives in a neighborhood, a community, a society.

Communication—interpersonal relationships—exists at all times in our lives. We constantly influence and are influenced by our environment. This is so even during times of bereavement.

In addition, some aspects of grief are common to all people, and draw meaning not from our own unique experience but from the common pool of universal experience. While occasional reference is made to "the reactions to this event by the remaining important family members,"[37] there has been very little exploration of either family or cultural influences on childhood bereavement.

Bereavement as Illness

Lastly, it is important to recognize that in the process of developing our understanding of bereavement we have reshaped, to some degree, what is a natural process into a form of pathology. While Freud clearly viewed bereavement as normal ("although grief involves grave departures from the normal attitude to life, it never occurs to us to regard it as a morbid condition and hand the mourner over to medical treatment"),[38] researchers and clinicians working with the bereaved since Freud's time have tended to focus on the pathological and thus, intentionally or unintentionally, have created a picture which emphasizes the disabling aspects of loss. We know more about the problems of coping with loss than about how people do cope, more about the social factors that inhibit grief and mourning than about those that promote it.

Summary

The purpose of this book is to examine sibling loss in childhood from the standpoint of family and cultural patterns of adaptation. While it is certainly true that intrapsychic processes play a significant role in affecting the outcome of adaptation to loss, this book focuses on the child's interactions with the world around him or her and how they either facilitate or hinder the process of coping. In this context, bereavement is viewed as a significant life event which calls for new modes of adaptation. The child's ability to adapt to the loss depends not only on his or her developmental stage, level of maturation, and ego functioning, but also on the relationships that exist between the child and many other individuals in his or her life. After the loss of a child, a family experiences a period of reorganization which reflects its adaptive strategies to cope with the loss and its resultant stress. These strategies will be communicated to the surviving siblings as messages about how to respond to the loss. Concerned friends and individuals outside the immediate family will also communicate messages to the child through their behavior in response to the loss. Further, a somewhat different picture emerges when bereavement is viewed from a cross-cultural perspective, which stresses the universal elements in response to death and how particular societies meet or fail to meet the needs of bereaved individuals that make up its members. All of these elements—family, social network, and cultural norms—play a significant role in determining the impact and outcome of sibling loss in childhood.

Children also "lose" a brother or sister through circumstances other than death. Each year a significant number of children are hospitalized, institutionalized, or placed in foster care for extended periods of time. Recently, a graduate student brought to my attention her concern about another group—children who remain behind in a foster home when one of their brothers or sisters is removed from it and placed somewhere else. How do families adapt to these changes? What kinds of communications are directed to the remaining siblings about the loss? What is society's role in response to these changes? Some of the issues are identical to those faced in sibling loss through death. While it is not within the scope of this book to study these events in detail, it is clear that all kinds of sibling loss are potentially significant in the life of a child. The ways in which children and their parents attempt to come to terms with these losses may color their behavior for the rest of their lives.

Notes

1. *Statistical Abstract of the United States,* 100th ed. (Washington, D.C.: U.S. Department of Commerce, Bureau of the Census, 1979), 73.

2. "Death Rate Increasing for Youths, Declining for Other Ages in U.S.," *New York Times,* 6 Dec. 1980, 1.

3. R. Gardner, "Children's Reactions to Parental Death," in *The Child and Death,* ed. J. Schowalter et al. (New York: Columbia University Press, 1983), 109.

4. Ibid.; B. Arthur and M. Kemme, "Bereavement in Childhood," *Journal of Child Psychology and Psychiatry* 5 (1964): 37–49; H. Nagera, "Children's Reactions to the Death of Important Objects," *Psychoanalytic Study of the Child* 25 (1970): 360–400, reprinted with permission; M. Barnes, "Reactions to the Death of a Mother," *Psychoanalytic Study of the Child* 19 (1964): 334–57.

5. E. Markusen and R. Fulton, "Childhood Bereavement and Behavior Disorders: A Critical Review," *OMEGA: Journal of Death and Dying* 2 (1971): 107–17.

6. M. Lewis and D. Lewis, "Dying Children and Their Families," in *The Child and Death,* ed. J. Schowalter et al. (New York: Columbia University Press, 1983), 137–55.

7. Nagera, "Children's Reactions to the Death of Important Objects," 365, reprinted with permission.

8. S. Freud, "Mourning and Melancholia," in *General Psychological Theory* (New York: Collier Books, 1963), 164–79.

9. D. Peretz, "Reaction to Loss," in *Loss and Grief: Psychological Management in Medical Practice,* ed. B. Schoenberg et al. (New York: Columbia University Press, 1970), 21.

10. J. Bowlby, "Childhood Mourning and Its Implications for Psychiatry," *American Journal of Psychiatry* 118 (1961): 481–98.

11. M. Wolfenstein, "How is Mourning Possible?" *Psychoanalytic Study of the Child* 21 (1966): 93–123.

12. R. Furman, "Death and the Young Child," *Psychoanalytic Study of the Child* 19 (1964): 321–33.

13. A. Freud, "Discussion of Dr. John Bowlby's Paper," *Psychoanalytic Study of the Child* 15 (1960): 53–62.

14. Ibid., 58.

15. G. Kliman, "Facilitation of Mourning During Childhood," in *Perspectives on Bereavement,* ed. I. Gerber (New York: Arno Press, 1979), 76–100; Gardner, "Children's Reactions to Parental Death," 106.

16. M. Nagy, "The Child's View of Death," in *The Meaning of Death,* ed. H. Feifel (New York: McGraw-Hill, 1959), 89–98.

17. J. Spinetta and P. Deasy-Spinetta, "Talking with Children Who Have a Life-threatening Illness," in *Living with Childhood Cancer,* ed. J. Spinetta and P. Deasy-Spinetta (St. Louis: C.V. Mosby, 1981), 234–52.

18. M. Bluebond-Langner, "Meanings of Death to Children," in *New Meanings of Death,* ed. H. Feifel (New York: McGraw-Hill, 1977), 47–66.

19. R. Gardner, personal conversation with author, 13 Aug. 1984, reprinted with permission.

20. D. Schell and C. Loder-McGough, "Children Also Grieve," in *Perspectives on Bereavement,* ed. I. Gerber (New York: Arno Press, 1977), 66.

21. R. Gardner, personal conversation with author, 13 Aug. 1984, reprinted with permission.

22. S. Bank and M. Kahn, *The Sibling Bond* (New York: Basic Books, 1982), 5.

23. G. Tsukada, "Sibling Interaction: A Review of the Literature," *Smith College Studies in Social Work* (1978): 229–47.

24. S. Rosenzweig and D. Bray, "Sibling Deaths in the Anamneses of Schizophrenic Patients," *Archives on Bereavement* (New York: Arno Press, 1979), 64–69.

25. H. Rosen and H. Cohen, "Children's Reactions to Sibling Loss," *Clinical Social Work Journal* 9, no. 3 (1981): 213.

26. L. Bender, *A Dynamic Psychopathology of Childhood* (Springfield, Ill.: Charles C. Thomas, 1954).

27. G. Pollock, "Childhood Parent and Sibling Loss in Adult Patients," *Archives of General Psychiatry* 7 (1962): 295–305; A. Cain, I. Fast, and M. Erickson, "Children's Disturbed Reaction to the Death of a Sibling," *American Journal of Orthopsychiatry* 34 (1964): 741–52.

28. B. Blinder, "Sibling Death in Childhood," *Child Psychiatry and Human Development* 2 (1972): 169–75.

29. Cain, Fast, and Erickson, "Children's Disturbed Reaction to the Death of a Sibling," 741–52.

30. D. Weston and R. Irwin, "Preschool Child's Response to Death of Infant Sibling," *American Journal of Diseases of Children* 106, no. 6 (1963): 564–67.

31. R. Krell and L. Rabkin, "The Effects of Sibling Death on the Surviving Child: A Family Perspective," *Family Process* 18, no. 4 (1979): 471–77.

32. Gardner, "Children's Reactions to Parental Death," 108.

33. Bank and Kahn, *The Sibling Bond*, 84–110.

34. B. Montalvo, personal conversation with author, 18 May 1984, reprinted with permission.

35. Ibid.

36. C. Parkes, *Bereavement—Studies of Grief in Adult Life* (New York: International University Press, 1972), 159–60.

37. Nagera, "Children's Reactions to the Death of Important Objects," 366, reprinted with permission.

38. Freud, "Mourning and Melancholia," 165.

2
Communication in the Bereaved Family: The Sibling Loss Survey

> Give sorrow words, the grief
> that does not speak
> Whispers the o'er-fraught heart
> and bids it break
>
> — Shakespeare, *Macbeth*

J ohn P. is the fourth of eight children born to a white, middle-class, Protestant family. Most of his childhood was spent on a small farm, where
he lived with his mother, father, and siblings. John's father, who was in
publishing, married John's mother just out of college, and they began a
family immediately. The first seven children were born within eleven years.
All but one were boys. The family lived on a tight budget, and the household
was cramped, crowded, and rather chaotic. Dinner was served in four shifts,
and in the summertime, the oldest four children slept on the porch. When
John was nine years old, his ten-year-old brother died in a shooting accident.
The members of John's family responded to the loss as if they were strangers
to one another. Years later, John recalls,

> I turned inside out with anguish and grief—and cried as never since. Then
> stricken into isolation, as if a buffer had fallen around me, I became acutely
> conscious of being alive, of life, and of the threat of death. . . . I felt removed
> from my parents and hungered to understand the secrecy of their grief. . . .
> Their withholding their own grief seemed like a removal of all parties to
> separate castles.

A writer now, John is able to express eloquently an experience that is widely
shared by many survivors of sibling loss and their families. A survey of adult
survivors of childhood sibling loss indicates that many families fail to communicate among themselves concerning the loss that they have experienced.
Siblings don't talk either to parents or to other siblings; parents don't communicate about the loss to each other or to their children.

The survey just mentioned was the initial phase of a project undertaken
to examine sibling loss in childhood. It focused on adults over the age of

fifteen who had experienced the loss of one or more siblings before the age of twenty. These "adult survivors" of sibling loss were asked to complete a survey questionnaire that focused on the circumstances of the loss and on their perceptions of how the loss had affected their lives and the lives of their families. The participants in the survey were recruited from a number of sources, including undergraduate and graduate classes at Rutgers University/ Camden, New Jersey, articles that were written in local newspapers around the country, and word of mouth. Close to 250 individuals were screened, and of these, 159 eventually completed the questionnaire. Seventeen states are represented in the survey population, with the largest samples coming from the greater Philadelphia and Boston areas. Since about 70 percent of the survey population was self-selected (volunteer), the representativeness of the survey population as a whole is unknown (see Appendix A for survey questionnaire).

Population Characteristics

The survey population was generally young, female, white, and married, with no children. Occupationally, professionals are heavily represented but not exclusively so. The participants resided primarily in three states—Massachusetts, New Jersey, and Pennsylvania. The Protestant religion was the most frequently cited affiliation, with a descending proportion of Catholics and Jews. Surviving siblings who were personally interviewed were highly representative of the survey population except in the areas of residence and occupation: interviews were limited to respondents from New Jersey and Pennsylvania, and since the Massachusetts sample was composed largely of professionals from that area, the elimination of this group from the interview sample affected information on occupational status also (see Appendix B for a complete socioeconomic profile of the survey population and Appendix C for the interview questionnaire).

Circumstances of Loss

Motor vehicle and other accidents were responsible for the largest percentage of sibling deaths (34 percent), followed by pneumonia, appendicitis, infections and related illnesses, and cancer. Forty-two percent of the surviving siblings were between the ages of six and twelve at the time their sibling died, and 27 percent of the siblings who died had also been in this age group. Sixty percent of the surviving siblings had lost an older sibling, and 64 percent had lost a brother (see Appendix D for complete data on circumstances of loss). While 41 percent of the respondents had learned of their sibling's death from their parents, a significant number (36 percent) learned of it through other sources, such as doctors, grandparents, or neighbors, or indirectly through overhearing parents talking on the telephone or doctors talking with relatives. Five percent of the surviving siblings were not told about the death when it occurred but learned of it years later through piecing together bits of information or asking questions. Most of the surviving siblings (77 percent) attended some or all of the services arranged for the sibling who died. Three-quarters of the surviving siblings had other brother(s) or sister(s) at the time of the death.

Initial Reactions to the Loss of a Sibling

Many people experience feelings of guilt over the death of a loved one, and children are no exception. In the survey, 50 percent of the surviving siblings reported feelings of guilt concerning their brother's or sister's death. Many children experienced guilt for being alive when their sibling died, for having been well when their sibling was ill, for past disagreements with their sibling, for having wished their sibling dead, and for feeling jealous of the parent's grief over the deceased sibling. Occasionally, surviving siblings reported having felt "special" because they had lost a brother or sister, and felt guilty because of this. When a child's illness had imposed restrictions on the healthy child's life, the latter often reported having felt angry, then guilty over the anger. And in their attempt to understand events around them, children often assign responsibility to themselves for events over which they have no control:

> I thought I had something to do with the cause of her death. We were playing on a bicycle and she fell off and got bruised. She had to go to the doctor's the next day for blood tests (nothing to do with the accident). She was put in a hospital immediately and came home only on weekends. She never got better.

> I . . . felt guilty for years that "it should have been me" rather than my brother who went to the store that day.

And following a suicide:

> I especially felt guilty because I felt responsible for his death. I had told Mama I would stay up that night and let my brother in when he came home from his date, but I didn't. I fell asleep instead. I didn't hear the doorbell and I didn't hear the gunshot . . . and I didn't hear Mama's scream. I felt I was somehow to blame for his death— and that if I had done what I had promised to do, then maybe my brother would not have killed himself. The guilt stayed with me longer than any of the other feelings.

The classical psychoanalytic understanding of guilt is that it is related to unconscious hostility, in this case directed toward the deceased sibling. In this context, the child feels that his own anger was in some way the cause of his sibling's death. Another way of understanding the emotion of guilt, suggested by Dr. Richard Gardner, is that it may be used as "an attempt to gain some control over this calamity, for personal control is strongly implied in the idea 'It's my fault.'"[1]

Of course, guilt is not the only emotion experienced when a sibling dies in childhood. Respondents to the study also reported feeling sad and hurt, lonely, angry, confused, frightened, disbelieving, apathetic, and numb. Many siblings fantasized that the "wrong one" died and felt their parents would not have grieved as much if they themselves had died instead.

While the surviving siblings in this study often reported having experienced intensely painful feelings surrounding the loss, the overwhelming majority said that they had shared their reactions with *no one*. Of the thirty four who were personally interviewed, twenty six (76 percent) reported that they had been unable to share their feelings with anyone at the time of the loss and largely thereafter. Only eight surviving siblings (24 percent) had talked with another person about how they felt at the time of their sibling's death. Of those eight, two spoke with a parent (one with mother, the other with father), two spoke with another sibling, and the remaining four spoke either with a therapist, cousin, aunt, or grandparents. In the survey, over 50 percent of the surviving siblings volunteered the information that they kept their feelings to themselves (they were not questioned directly about this). The tendency of surviving siblings not to share their feelings with others was not influenced by their age at the time of their sibling's death, the age at which their sibling died, the socioeconomic circumstances of their family, including ethnicity, the size of their family, or their birth order in the family. Only one factor showed any correlation at all to expressiveness or lack thereof over the loss, and that was religion. One half of the surviving siblings who reported sharing their feelings at the time of the loss were Catholic, compared to only one quarter of those who did not. Of the total number of respondents who did not share their feelings with anyone, the most commonly reported religious affiliation was Protestant (42 percent), with another 27 pecent being Jewish. While it appears then that Catholic children may be more expressive of how they feel when a sibling dies, this finding must be viewed with caution, owing to the small size of the sample making up the group who shared their feelings at the time of the loss.

Finally, many of the surviving siblings (approximately one-third) reported feeling a responsibility or need to comfort one or even both parents. This feeling took precedence over the need to express their own feelings of loss and was often coupled with a sense of having to make up to the parents for the loss of a child. In one sense, this may be viewed as a kind of vicarious consolation through which the child may also be able to console his or her projected self. Still, as surviving siblings describe it, the loss of opportunity for direct expression of their own feelings is of major consequence. A few examples from the survey illustrate:

> The brother of a twelve-year-old girl died suddenly after being struck by a truck. She responded: "I was very worried about how my parents were feeling and felt that if I ever let all my sadness and grief show it would make things worse for them. I never talked to them about my feelings. [Today] I feel more [of a] sense of obligation to both my parents and my brothers. With my parents, it's mostly that I'm so aware of all they've been through, and only recently have I been able to stop trying to 'make it up to them.'"

A thirteen-year-old girl lost her brother to leukemia:

> I tried to be real good, grownup so as not to get my parents upset. I took charge, helped clean out his things, and moved into his room. I tried very hard to do everything right—not to create any waves for them. I pretended it didn't happen.

A useful way of understanding this feeling of responsibility may be found in the concept of the family "legacy." This consists of an ethical demand that derives from the parent/child relationship. It begins with the child's debt to the parent for life itself and implies that a child "owes" the parent for his or her existence. Extenuating circumstances may increase the child's debt:

> Not every family has to survive under excessive degrees of extenuating circumstances. Yet, in certain families most members were wiped out by the holocaust. In other families several consecutive generations lost their mothers at an early age. . . . Early death of several siblings or the birth of a brain-damaged sibling can constitute rapid escalation of over-weighted legacies, which calls for an existential rebalancing of the unfair destiny of the family and its members.[2]

It should be stressed that the legacy is not psychological but rather is an existential given—a fact of life that each individual contends with. Over-weighted legacies or difficulties in making "payment" can be damaging to a child and can create pathogenic relationships throughout the family. The "invisible establishment" or rules that govern family behavior may contribute to difficulties in maintaining balance in family relationships by disallowing members to behave assertively. Assertion and individuation may be viewed as demonstrations of disloyalty under these circumstances.

Boszormenyi-Nagy's theory of the family legacy bears directly on the experience of sibling loss. It appears from the survey data that for some families the loss of even one sibling raised ethical and existential issues for surviving siblings, especially around the felt need to repay the parents for their loss. Since this is in fact impossible to do, these surviving siblings and their families may need help in rebalancing the family ledger and reestablishing a sense of family fairness.

Parental Grief Reactions

Evidence indicates that the death of a child is the most difficult loss for an adult to sustain.[3] Sanders, for example, in comparing reactions to the loss of a spouse, child, or parent, found that "those who experienced the death of a child revealed more intense grief reactions of somatic types, greater depression, as well as anger and guilt with accompanying feelings of despair, than did those bereaved who had experienced the death of either a spouse or parent."[4] When a child becomes ill with a life-threatening illness, the parents are often viewed as "hurting" as much or even more than their ill child (thus, for example, the chapter heading "The Parents of the Child with Cancer: A View from Those Who Suffer Most" in a book about childhood cancer).[5] There are cultural variations, nevertheless, in parental grief responses to the loss of a child. For the Aymara of Bolivia, for example, the death of a child is followed by much less sadness and ceremony than is the death of an older person. Stillborn infants are simply disposed of.[6]

There is a large degree of cross-cultural similarity, though, in expression of grief by women and men. In a small number of cultures studied, men and women are equal in their expression of this emotion, but many societies exhibit sex-based differences in this area. In all societies in which sex-based differences have been observed, women cry more than men, while men are more frequent in their expression of anger. Rosenblatt, Walsh, and Jackson write:

> Although there is a substantial amount of similarity between men and women in emotionality during bereavement, there is consistency across cultures in the pattern of sex differences. . . . Women seem to cry, to attempt self-mutilation, and actually to self-mutilate more than men; men seem to show more anger and aggression directed away from self.[7]

Possible reasons for these differences include deeper attachments developed by women, different patterns of socialization, and a greater propensity among women to engage in help-seeking and crying behaviors.

With regard to the research study, many surviving siblings reported differences in the expression of grief by their parents. Thirty-three percent of respondents reported that their mothers experienced a prolonged depression or withdrawal from the family following the loss of their sibling, and forty two (27 percent) reported observing depression and/or distancing in their fathers. Typically, the surviving siblings' mothers were more expressive of their feelings of grief, whereas their fathers exhibited withdrawal, anger, and suppression of feelings more extensively. The following excerpts illustrate:

Carol G. was eight when her six-year-old sister died in an automobile accident. Her mother was pregnant at the time and gave birth the day after her sibling's funeral. Shortly thereafter, Mrs. G. became profoundly depressed and was hospitalized for three months, during which time Carol lived with different sets of relatives. Neither Carol nor her mother attended the funeral for her sister.

Barbara T. was twelve when her sixteen-year-old sister died of cancer. Following the death, her mother would not allow her sister's clothes, jewelry, and other personal items to be removed for over three years. At the same time, Mrs. T. cried freely and said, "What do I have to live for now?"

Ann S. was thirteen years old when her nine-year-old brother died in a drowning accident. Her father pulled away from the family emotionally and was never as close to his remaining children again, stating that he never wanted to be hurt that much. Mr. S. tried to make his son's room into a shrine and became angry when the surviving siblings took mementos of their brother.

A woman who had lost her seven-year-old sibling in an unusual playground accident wrote:

In a way, my mother never recovered from losing her seven-year-old daughter. I don't know how you ever can truly get over something like that, but I know she could have made some more peace with it. I talked to her for the first time about my sister some ten years after her death. At the mention of her name, my mother cried like the death had just happened—it is still so raw for her.

Parental grief over the loss of a child may be a factor in altering long-standing patterns of coping within a family. In all families, patterns evolve over time which include systems of alliances ("She's her father's daughter") and ways of coping (the oldest daughter helping the mother to raise the younger siblings) that are functional for the family and that form a part of each family's style or character. The death of a child can significantly alter these patterns, resulting in new ones that are either functional or, at times, highly dysfunctional. For example, in one family, the death of an older sibling whose roles had included that of negotiator between the parents and younger siblings resulted in a dysfunctional relationship between the mother and the surviving child, a daughter. The following excerpt illustrates:

> Mary R. was fifteen when her twenty-year-old brother died from leukemia. Mark had been the buffer between Mary and her overly protective, somewhat intrusive mother. Mark's interceptions on Mary's behalf had allowed greater autonomy and [more] appropriate peer relations than would have been the case otherwise. After Mark's death, Mary became the sole object of her mother's concern and control. The remainder of Mary's adolescence was characterized by intense battles between Mary and her mother and premature marriage at age eighteen to escape parental dominance.

Communication and Adaptation in the Bereaved Family

In view of the preceding material, it would not be surprising to discover that communication among family members around the death of the sibling is severely limited, and, in fact, this was often the case for families described in the study. In analyzing the 159 survey responses, the theme of lack of communication among family members following the death of a child was found in 27 percent of the questionnaires. But when specifically asked whether the family had ever discussed the death of the sibling, 62 percent (21) of the surviving siblings who were interviewed said no, 26 percent (9) said yes, and 12 percent (4) said occasionally. Communication in these families was not influenced by the age of the child who had died or by the cause of death, family size (number of children), the age of the parents at the time of the death, or the family's socioeconomic circumstances. Once again, though, religion was a factor, in that of those families that discussed the loss, only 24 percent were Catholic, whereas 52 percent were Protestant. Put another way, one out of two Catholic families that lost a child talked about it, whereas only one out of twelve Protestant families did the same, and only one out of five Jewish families. If we combine "occasionally" with "yes," the comparable percentages for Protestant, Catholic, and Jewish families that talked about the loss are 17 percent, 50 percent, and 25 percent, respectively. In the case of John's family, the lack of communication was one factor that served to hinder the family in establishing new patterns of coping. His next younger brother, who physically resembled the sibling who had died, moved into the room that John had formerly shared with his deceased brother. John silently resented this younger brother's presence as "the reincarnation of a threat that had died," and at the same time feared that his anger would precipitate a new disaster. Since John's mother became severely depressed and drank heavily after the loss of his brother, his older and only sister became a substitute mother, to some degree. The marriage became brittle and the parents' attempt to replace the lost child resulted in the birth of a Down's syndrome baby who was named after the deceased sibling. While John felt he had inherited expectations of academic excellence previously fulfilled by his deceased sibling, he rebelled against them, determinedly remaining an average student. The legacy of John's loss can already be traced to a new generation in that his experience of parenthood brought on inappropriate fear concerning his daughter's well-being. The normal frustrations of parenthood snowballed into intolerable anxiety and formed the impetus for John to seek counseling. He has since become aware of the degree to which his daughter became a replacement for the brother who had died.[8]

Taboos and Ties

The family's inability to communicate about the loss of a child is reminiscent of the taboo against uttering the name of a dead person that is found in many cultures throughout the world. In *Totem and Taboo*, Freud mentioned fourteen societies, including those of the Australians, Polynesians, some tribes of Africa, and inhabitants of Borneo, Madagascar, and Tasmania, in which customs of this kind have existed. He wrote:

> This custom is extremely widespread, it is expressed in a variety of ways and has had important consequences. . . . The avoidance of the name of a dead person is a rule enforced with extreme severity.[9]

In some cultures, people with names the same as or similar to the name of the deceased will change their name. Freud wrote that in Paraguay, "the dread of uttering a dead person's name extends, indeed, to an avoidance of the mention of anything in which the dead man played a part; and an important consequence of this process of suppression is that these peoples possess no tradition and no historical memory."[10] Compare that description to this statement from a study respondent: "After [one reference to my brother] I never heard my mother mention my brother's name again or refer to him in any way. In fact, no one in my family or school or at church would talk about my brother. It was almost as though he had never existed." In some societies, the names of the deceased are revived after many years and are given to children who are then considered reincarnations of the dead.

Freud traced the earliest reasoning behind the taboo to the cultural belief in demons. Some societies believe that after death, the loved one is transformed into a demon whom one may unwittingly evoke through use of his name. Continuing his speculations, Freud suggested that the so-called demons are projections of the survivors' own hostile feelings toward the deceased. Since all relationships have a certain degree of ambivalence, some hostility is always present in our feelings toward others, living or dead.

Others suggest a different purpose behind the taboo—that of assisting the bereaved in the necessary task of breaking ties with the deceased. Concerning the loss of a spouse, Rosenblatt, Walsh, and Jackson write:

> In many societies, there are death customs which eliminate reminders of a deceased spouse during the bereavement period. . . . The customs include destroying, giving away, or temporarily putting aside personal property of the deceased, observing a taboo on the name of the deceased, and changing residence.[11]

The tie-breaking activities noted in the preceding extract, and particularly the taboo on the name of the deceased, are in contradiction to many prevailing theories in this country that regard the expression of feelings (catharsis) as valuable to the process of working through the experience of loss. To a great degree, we believe that expressing grief, and using the name of the deceased as well, is necessary for working through grief. Any avoidance of this activity could arrest or postpone working through the loss. The opposing theory suggested by Rosenblatt, Walsh, and Jackson is that tie-breaking activities aid in the working-through process by reducing the amount of habitual behavior that has to be changed. Through eliminating reminders of the deceased, a new environment is created that will avoid eliciting behaviors formerly associated with that person. In an extreme form of the coping response, some families will change their residence and even geographic locale in attempting to break ties to the family member who died.

Summary

In general, then, this exploration of family members' responses to the loss of a child has examined individual reactions of siblings and parents, communication about the loss between family members, and behavioral adaptations of the family to the loss of a role fulfiller. In the survey on sibling loss, surviving siblings reported feelings of guilt, sadness, loneliness, anger, confusion, fear, disbelief, and numbness and often did not share their feelings with any other person. They frequently felt the need to comfort their parents and to make up to them for the loss. Typically, mothers were more expressive of their grief than fathers, who tended to withdraw or exhibit angry behavior, or do both. In the survey population, there was little open communication reported among family members regarding the death. Yet, alterations in family interactions and the loss of a role fulfiller often caused new and dysfunctional family patterns.

From a cross-cultural perspective, taboos and tie-breaking behaviors suggest that much of what a bereaved family experiences is felt universally. We may be moved to respond to loss by currents that run deeper than either individual or family experience can completely account for. In examining patterns of communication and adaptation, we have observed some families in which there is a high risk for the development of pathology because parents are unable to recover from the loss. In these circumstances, the family life cycle becomes frozen, and there is an inability to nurture surviving siblings. These are families in which the loss of a child breeds pathology for the future of the entire family.

In the next chapter, we will explore the responses of the bereaved community—friends, neighbors, and teachers—to the loss, and ways in which these responses can either support or further isolate surviving family members in their grief.

Notes

1. R. Gardner, "The Guilt Reactions of Parents of Children with Severe Physical Disease," *American Journal of Psychiatry* 126, no. 5 (1969): 82.

2. I. Boszormenyi-Nagy, "Behavior Change Through Family Change," in *What Makes Behavior Change Possible,* ed. A. Burton (New York: Bruner/Mazel, 1976), 242.

3. G. Owen, R. Fulton, and E. Markusen, "Death at a Distance: A Study of Family Survivors," *OMEGA: Journal of Death and Dying* 13, no. 3 (1982–83): 191–225.

4. C. Sanders, "A Comparison of Adult Bereavement in the Death of a Spouse, Child and Parent," *OMEGA: Journal of Death and Dying* 10, no. 4 (1979–80): 309.

5. J. Spinetta and P. Deasy-Spinetta, *Living with Childhood Cancer* (St. Louis: C.V. Mosby, 1981).

6. M. Diskin and H. Guggenheim, "The Child and Death as Seen in Different Cultures," in *Explaining Death to Children,* ed. E. Grollman (Boston: Beacon Press, 1967), 111–26.

7. P. Rosenblatt, R. Walsh, and D. Jackson, *Grief and Mourning in Cross-cultural Perspective* (HRAF Press, 1976), 24.

8. See, for example, M. Selvini Palazzoli, "The Problem of the Sibling as the Referring Person," *Journal of Marital and Family Therapy* 2, no. 1 (1985): 21–34.

9. S. Freud, *Totem and Taboo* (New York: Standard Edition, 1952), 54.

10. Ibid., 55–56.

11. Rosenblatt, Walsh, and Jackson, *Grief and Mourning in Cross-cultural Perspective,* 68.

3
Society and the Bereaved Family

Kathy R. is the younger of two children born to a Virginia farming family. Her brother was born two years after Mr. and Mrs. R. were married; Kathy arrived four years later. Kathy grew up in a small house less than 100 yards from her paternal grandparents. Her grandfather worked as a farmer, and her grandmother was a teacher in a one-room country school. Kathy's father was an only son, so his parents did not offer to send him to college as they had his sister—instead, they offered him a half interest in the farm. During the depression, such an opportunity for security was not to be ignored, and Kathy's father rather reluctantly became a farmer. Her mother was a full-time homemaker until Kathy became thirteen. She did not particularly care for the life of a farmer's wife and suffered migraine headaches in hot weather.

Kathy was nineteen years old when her brother died in a mining accident. The roof of the mine in which he had been working to defray his college costs collapsed. He was the only casualty.

Kathy experienced his death in many ways. Today when she looks back at the loss, some of her strongest feelings concern the reactions that others had toward her and her loss and the influence these reactions had on her response to her brother's death both at the time it occurred and continuing up to the present. She states:

> I've spent so long denying my feelings of loss that that is the truth. I have little feeling of loss that I'm aware of. All the messages that my loss was trivial have "won." I'm now aware of a fair amount of anger about that. At the time it felt like everyone else had made the judgment that my loss was relatively trivial and therefore I should support my parents through their mourning. Since so much time has elapsed I feel like I was denied the opportunity to deal with my feelings at the appropriate time and as a result find them interfering with my life. Now all the years of dealing with my brother as a "ghost" are there, and I don't think I can think about the loss itself.

The foregoing quotation demonstrates that the human mind stores and assimilates information and attitudes from multiple sources. Ways of perceiving the world developed in one context inevitably become "part of the person's approach to the current context with which he interacts."[1] The past is always part of the present.

While the family is a primary source for the accumulation of information and attitudes, institutions and social networks outside the family also play a significant role. It is a mistake to assume that only close family members affect our view of the world:

> Less significant others function as a sort of chorus. . . . The relation between the significant others and the "chorus" in reality-maintenance is a dialectical one; that is, they interact with each other as well as with the subjective reality they serve to confirm.[2]

Conversation is the most important vehicle by which an individual's subjective reality is maintained, modified, and reconstructed by others. Conversation "gives firm contours to items previously apprehended in a fleeting and unclear manner."[3] Lack of conversation about something may weaken one's very belief in it, since "the subjective reality of something that is never talked about comes to be shaky."[4] For Kathy, the very essence of the experience of loss was altered at least partially by the responses of individuals outside the immediate family. Her report was not unique in this respect; many of the survey respondents related similar experiences.

Responses from the Bereaved Community

Individuals outside the immediate family comprise what we shall call the bereaved community. An analysis of the questionnaires revealed thirty-two (20 percent) responses from such individuals. Thirty of the references were negative in that the surviving siblings experienced the exchanges (all of them verbal, but some avoiding conversation about the loss) as increasing their aloneness and sense of isolation. In only two instances were the interactions felt to be helpful. Members of the bereaved community included peers; neighbors and adult friends of the family; aunts, uncles, and cousins; grandparents; police; teachers; and religious representatives. Table 3–1 shows the number of responses reported for each group. In general, reported comments from the bereaved community fell into two categories. A discussion of each follows.

Table 3–1
Responses from Bereaved Community

	Number of Times Reported
Neighbors and adult friends	10
Teachers	9
Peers	4
Aunts, uncles, cousins	3
Grandparents	2
Police	1
Religious representatives	1

Admonitions to Be Strong

In the first category were statements made to the surviving sibling that conveyed the idea "Be strong for your parents." Three examples follow, the first from a young woman whose brother was stabbed:

> When my brother was killed, I was constantly being asked about my mother, told to take care of her, and the one thing I resented most of all was the "be strong for her" lectures I got. No one seemed to recognize my loss. People only saw the death of her son, not my brother.

Another woman, who lost her brother during World War II, reported:

> I felt an extreme loss that no one else seemed to understand. All the relatives paid all the attention to my folks. One aunt by marriage told me not to cry, for my parents' sake. I was very bewildered.

Even a brief encounter with the police may be significant in getting the message across:

> I was home sick from school when two policemen came to the door looking for my mother, who was at work. They told me it was about my sister, but wouldn't say what except that I had better get dressed as my mother may need me.

The message to be strong may have been motivated by the adults' concern for the distraught parents or by their own need not to see the child unhappy. Gardner feels that overprotective parents (and I extend this to overprotective members of the bereaved community) "may operate on the principle that everything must be done to prevent the child from experiencing pain."[5] Thus, the protective approach, which will be discussed in greater detail in chapter 4, dictates that children must be spared the pain of confrontation with mortality. For some, it is a personal ethic that dictates the response, such as the belief that one gets stronger by bearing pain without flinching.

Silence

In the second category were responses that indicated to surviving siblings that their own loss was totally ignored. The silence of others was often felt to be a clear message to the child that he or she had not undergone a significant bereavement experience. Teachers, more than any other group, were cited in this category. For example:

> I felt very alone because no one knew how I felt and my teacher told the other kids not to talk to me about my sister's death (they told me she said not to mention it).

> I turned inside out with anguish and grief—and cried as never since. Then, stricken into isolation, as if a buffer had fallen around me. . . . By elders—parents and teachers—I felt misunderstood and neglected, and somehow abused.

Not surprisingly, some surviving siblings even felt betrayed by peers. A woman whose twin brother died in his early teens reported:

> Immediately following his death, it was very difficult to concentrate [in school]. In addition, as we were in the same class with the same friends, many children avoided contact with me and treated me differently, as they didn't know how I would react at any given time.

The role of the bereaved community appears to be twofold: first, statements made by these individuals to a surviving sibling may further underline the latter's sense that his or her loss is not real, and second, lack of conversation about the surviving sibling's loss is experienced as a missed opportunity, that is, as neglect of the sibling's needs by someone in a position to help. This is a prime example of the "social pathology of mourning" in operation. The bereaved individual is isolated, avoided, scrupulously treated as though nothing had happened. While the intention may be only to avoid reference to the loss itself, the result may be little interaction with the bereaved community about anything at all, since conversation entails the risk that the distressing subject of the death will arise. There are a number of possible explanations for this behavior.

Isolation of the Bereaved

At the individual level, the inability of members of the bereaved community to communicate to surviving siblings about the loss of a brother or a sister may be a defense against their own death anxiety. To some degree, we all use denial as a defense against the fear that death evokes. Fear of death may be synonymous with fear of pain, separation, or loss of self. Denial as a defense against death anxiety is believed by many to be a characteristic response in our society.[6]

When we again look at the cross-cultural perspective, we find that the taboo on speaking the name of the deceased is carried out not just by the bereaved family itself but also by the wider society surrounding the bereaved family. Rosenblatt, Walsh, and Jackson found that the taboo generally applies to "close kinsmen of the deceased or to *people in their presence*" (italics added).[7] In a small number of societies, the taboo applies to all members of the community. In fact, the customs and ceremonies surrounding death often dictate other behaviors for the society as a whole, because death, through the complex and contradictory emotions it evokes, threatens the solidarity and very existence of every society.[8] Horror and fear of death have always aroused the instinct of self-preservation—"to abandon the corpse, to run away from the village, to destroy all the belongings of the dead one."[9] These impulses have been in existence throughout history,

> and if given way to would be extremely dangerous, disintegrating the group, destroying the material foundations of primitive culture. . . . By setting in motion one part of the deep forces of the instinct of self-preservation, it threatens the very cohesion and solidarity of the group, and upon this depends the organization of that society, its tradition, and finally the whole culture. For if primitive man yielded always to the disintegrating impulses of his reaction to death, the continuity of tradition and the existence of material civilization would be made impossible.[10]

Isolation of the bereaved may also be viewed as a means through which societies can control anger and aggression.[11] Feelings of anger are commonly experienced by bereaved individuals and are often observed by those close to the bereaved, who are usually surprised and perhaps puzzled by these feelings. From a cultural standpoint, anger and aggression are disruptive and can be dangerous to the community's very existence; excessive anger must be controlled if a society is to survive. Isolating the bereaved is one way to ensure that untoward incidents will not trigger an aggressive episode. As one of the surviving siblings quoted earlier remarked, "Many children avoided contact with me and treated me differently, as they didn't know how I would react at any given time."

Summary

It is possible, then, to interpret the social isolation experienced by bereaved children in at least three ways. Members of the bereaved community involved with the death of a child may avoid mentioning the death because (1) they need to construct a defense against their own death anxiety, (2) they feel that surviving siblings need to be spared the pain of confrontation with death, and (3) they are responding out of a universally felt need to protect the social order from the potential chaos, anger, and aggression that loss creates in the bereaved and those close to the bereaved. These responses may find support in certain ethical prescriptions which promote the processes of denial and suppression.

Up to this point, we have been examining primarily the social pathology of sibling loss. In the next chapter, we will look at some of the ways children cope with the loss and adapt to their new reality.

Notes

1. S. Minuchin, *Families and Family Therapy* (Cambridge: Harvard University Press, 1984), 6.

2. P.L. Berger and T. Luckmann, *The Social Construction of Reality* (Garden City, N.Y.: Doubleday and Company, 1966), 151.

3. Ibid., 153.

4. Ibid.

5. R. Gardner, "Children's Reactions to Parental Death," in *The Child and Death*, ed. J. Schowalter et al. (New York: Columbia University Press, 1983), 114.

6. R. Dumont and D. Foss, *The American View of Death* (Cambridge: Schenkman Publishing Co., 1972).

7. P. Rosenblatt, R. Walsh, and D. Jackson, *Grief and Mourning in Cross-cultural Perspective* (HRAF Press, 1976), 76.

8. B. Malinowski, *Magic, Science and Religion* (Glencoe, Ill.: Free Press, 1948), 48.

9. Ibid.

10. Ibid., 52–53.

11. Rosenblatt, Walsh, and Jackson, *Grief and Mourning in Cross-cultural Perspective*, 77.

4
Coping with the Death of a Child

S ally C. is a bright, vivacious twenty-four-year-old woman who lives and
works in Philadelphia. Her parents, both Philadelphians, met on a blind
date and were married soon afterward, at the same time her father en-
tered law school. Her mother, a bookkeeper, worked until she became pregnant with Sally's older brother, Mike. Sally was born four years later.

Sally describes her family as having been poor but happy during her early
years. She and her brother enjoyed an unusual amount of freedom and became close friends. Sally was included in almost all of Mike's activities, including baseball and football games and fishing expeditions. Sally's mother
was the troop leader for Mike's Boy Scouts troop, and Sally was included in
those activities as well. In addition, the family was surrounded by extended
family and spent a good deal of time with grandparents, aunts, uncles, and
cousins.

One day when Sally was eight, Mike was hit by a car as he was walking
along the road. He was not killed instantly but remained in a coma until his
death four years later. Sally recalls that around the time of the accident,

> My parents never said anything to me about [it], just that Mike was in the
> hospital and was getting better. Mostly life went on. I was completely shel-
> tered from everything. One day I went to my Mom and asked when Mike
> was coming home. He was my best friend and life was a bit dull without
> him. A lot of this time is pretty hazy, but I remember that night. Dad was
> working late, not a common occurrence. I was eating a large plate of noodles
> and tomato sauce, my favorite meal. Mom said he was never coming home
> again. I remember crying and crying. It is one of the last times in my life I
> cried. I was eight.

Sally visited her brother in the hospital on only one occasion. She was
angry when she saw that his hair had been cut, since he liked to wear it long.
Because she was told that Mike was now deaf, dumb, and blind, she read
everything she could find on Helen Keller and learned the manual alphabet

to teach him. At home, she tried to keep things in order for him, retrieving records he had loaned to friends and ripping off the months on his calendar. She also drew pictures for him to have in the hospital.

While Sally and her parents never discussed Mike's condition at home, Sally feels that during the time Mike was in the hospital, she became resigned to his absence. She recalls feeling very little emotion at his death. For her, he had already died.

Sally's situation was unusual compared with that of most respondents to the survey in that her brother lived for four years in a state of coma and, as a result, she was able to realize he was gone and accept the fact of his absence gradually, over that period of time. By the time he died, she had to some extent already mourned the loss. During the four-year period, Sally also engaged in a variety of activities that helped her understand and cope with the loss. She tried to help her brother by learning a way to communicate with him; she managed his affairs in his absence; and she kept track of the passing time. These endeavors also helped her to experience, in limited doses, the grief associated with her brother's death.

For Kathy R., whom we met in chapter 3, the death of her brother was sudden and dramatic and afforded her no time to prepare for acceptance of the loss. Her ways of attempting to cope with the stress of the loss included riding her bicycle five or six hours a day, isolating herself, escaping into sleeping binges lasting between sixteen and twenty hours a day, abusing alcohol, and hitting walls. Mementos—especially clothing—also played a large role in helping her to cope. Her brother had given her a few sweaters, and she also had one of his that he had outgrown. Although she had little conscious awareness of how important the sweaters were to her, she was significantly depressed when they were lost in moving. She hadn't bought herself a sweater since his death.

It is generally believed that when there is a loss of a significant person in the life of a child, the expression of feelings—guilt, anger, anxiety—is helpful and should be allowed and encouraged.[1] It is also known that after experiencing such a death, children sometimes cry and appear grief-stricken and sometimes do not. There are frequent references in the literature to examples of bereaved children's behavior that seem to indicate lack of grief or a grief of short duration.[2] At the present time, however, we lack an adequate understanding of the resources that children employ in coping with a significant loss in their lives.

Grief and Mourning in Adulthood

In the case of adult bereavement, there is general agreement on what constitutes healthy responses to loss. Rosenblatt, Walsh, and Jackson state that "the experience of grief seems to be one of the costs of being human"[3]—that is, the experience of grief and mourning following upon loss is universal. Gardner points out that we also "benefit" from the capacity to grieve in that our ability to mourn is intrinsically related to our understanding that life is time-limited and special. Without this understanding, we would forfeit much of the richness of life.[4]

In most cultures, it is deemed essential that adult survivors "work-through" a loss, a process that includes three related elements.[5] First, the bereaved individual must accept the reality of the loss, that is, he or she must acknowledge that the death has occurred. It is not uncommon for a person to react to the initial news of a death with disbelief, but this reaction must give way to an acknowledgment of the reality of the death before mourning can occur.

Second, behaviors associated with the deceased must be altered. Extinction of behaviors that are no longer adaptive is essential to the process of working through grief. If a mother, for instance, continues to maintain the room of a deceased child as if that child were still living in it, she is failing to adapt to her changed reality.

Third, feelings of guilt, anger, and other emotions associated with the loss must dissipate. For most persons, time and the grieving process serve to lessen the intensity of emotion surrounding a loss. When this does not occur, an individual continues to react to thoughts of the deceased with intense and painful emotions. Social customs regarding responses to loss assist individuals in making the transition from mourner to nonmourner. When viewed cross-culturally, both grief and mourning in adults, along with postdeath rituals, show a striking similarity throughout the world. Unfortunately, we still lack comparable data on loss in childhood. The tendency to view children as somehow immune from bereavement has resulted in a significant lack of data from which to theorize. The effort made in this book is only a step in the opposite direction, and it is hoped that what is revealed here will stimulate further investigation into the crucial subject of childhood bereavement.

Coping Behaviors

Table 4–1 lists behaviors that surviving siblings found useful in coping with the death of a brother or sister. The number of times behaviors were reported and the ages or age range in which they occurred are shown as well. The table does not make up a definitive list of coping activities but gives an indication of some of the activities young people find helpful in coping with sibling loss.

Immersing oneself in schoolwork or school-related activities was the most frequently mentioned behavior and it was reported by adolescents be-

Table 4–1
Coping Behaviors of Surviving Siblings

Behavior	Number of Times Reported	Age of Sibling
1. Focusing on schoolwork and/or school-related activities	8	13–17
2. Keeping an object, article of clothing, or toy of the deceased	7	4–16
3. Sibling's religious faith, saying prayers	6	5–17
4. Attending services for the deceased	5	4–8, 15
5. Observing grief and support of community, friends, family	5	12–14
6. Crying when alone	3	7–12
7. Engaging in fate-provoking behavior	2	10, 15
8. Talking with therapist	2	17, 18
9. Writing "dead" on coloring book	1	10
10. Observing parents' religious faith	1	14
11. Looking at pictures of deceased	1	7
12. Maintaining normal routine	1	12

tween the ages of thirteen and seventeen. The demands of continued academic performance were sometimes experienced as an added strain, a pressure to excel that the child felt unable to deal with. The dichotomy regarding the role of schoolwork has also been reported in relation to children with siblings who have cancer.[6] It appears to be a common theme in response both to significant loss and to the threat of loss, and therefore suggests that there is a need for great sensitivity on the part of school personnel in order to differentiate the needs of one child from another.

Retaining an article of clothing, toy, or some other object that belonged to the deceased was reported with the second greatest frequency and across a wide age span of four to sixteen. This behavior took place even in the context of family opposition, or when the parents' intention or behavior was to discard the belongings of the deceased. That these articles are symbols or substitutes for the deceased sibling is clear both to the surviving sibling and to the child's parents—they serve as a link or a tie to the deceased. Yet the survey evidence indicates that the inclination regarding what to do with such articles may be quite different for parents and surviving siblings in their mutual efforts to cope with the loss.

Saying prayers or drawing upon religious faith was the third most frequently reported means of coping. Some respondents reported that the death of a sibling raised serious religious doubts in their minds or anger at God. Similarly, attending services for the deceased and observing and/or touching the body of the deceased was helpful for some children but frightening for others. As Wessel comments in relation to the death of a parent, a child may find the gathering of friends and the ritual of services either supportive or more than he or she can cope with.[7]

Observing the grief of others and experiencing the support of community, friends, and family was reported as helpful in five cases, all within the age range of twelve to fourteen. This category included both peers and adult community members who indicated through their behavior that the loss was significant to them as well.

Two respondents reported what could be labeled "fate-provoking behavior" following the death of their siblings. In one instance, a teenager whose brother had died in a diving accident subsequently dove into the same swimming pool at the same time of day as the sibling had when he died. This behavior appeared to satisfy the surviving sibling's need for reassurance that his brother's fate would not befall him. In a second instance, a surviving sibling's younger brother had been hit by a truck while she and he were walking to school together. One day soon afterward, a neighbor requested that the surviving sibling walk her own son to school. The surviving sibling experienced this as an important indication of her continued worth despite the tragic accident.

Two older surviving siblings, aged seventeen and eighteen, spoke with therapists after the death of their siblings. One surviving sibling reported going through the pages of his deceased brother's coloring book and writing "dead" on each page. Other surviving siblings reported attending services for their sibling, crying when alone, observing their parents' religious faith, looking at pictures of the deceased, and maintaining their normal routine as aids in coping with the loss.

Working through Childhood Bereavement

Earlier in the chapter, we discussed the three elements of working through bereavement that are generally accorded importance for bereaved adults. The elements are (1) acceptance of the loss, (2) extinction of behaviors that are no longer adaptive, and (3) dissipation of guilt, anger, and other disruptive emotions. One of the major differences in the bereavement experience for children is the state of dependency which characterizes them and the threat to their security which death poses. A surviving sibling may feel threatened by his parents' grief and possible unavailability and by the fear that he may also die. Children's grief "is bound up with the fear of the loss of their security."[8]

One can postulate, then, that some of the behaviors of bereaved children may be directed at increasing their sense of security and minimizing threats to their daily life. Assuming that the elements of working through bereavement that are required for adults are necessary for children as well, we can now list four behaviors which we might expect to see in bereaved children:

1. behaviors which aid the child in accepting the reality of the loss
2. behaviors which assist the child in letting go of behaviors that are no longer appropriate
3. behaviors which assist the child in coping with the powerful feelings engendered by the loss
4. behaviors which help the child maintain a sense of continuity and safety in the world

Using these behaviors as the basis for a taxonomy, we can categorize them according to their function in helping the surviving sibling to cope with the loss of a sister or brother (see table 4–2). Categories are not mutually exclusive: some behaviors can be observed to fill more than one function. It is also probable that behaviors fill varying functions for different children. Nevertheless, viewing a child's behavior in terms of how it meets the child's needs to cope and adapt establishes a framework that serves as a first step toward greater clarity in the subject of childhood bereavement. The assumption behind this view is that the behaviors that children elect do in fact serve a useful function in helping them to cope with their loss.

Behaviors whose function is to dissipate disruptive emotions were reported most frequently, and behaviors whose function is to extinguish responses that are no longer adaptive received the least frequent mention. The so-called tie-breaking activities (that is, behaviors such as discarding personal property that serve to eliminate reminders of the deceased) were notably absent from surviving siblings' reports. In fact, as we saw earlier, *retaining* articles of the deceased was reported as a helpful coping activity even, at times, in the face of parental wishes to do the opposite. In chapters 2 and 3, we noted that avoiding speaking the name of the deceased (another tie-breaking activity) was observed to be more predominant among adults in and close to the bereaved family than among surviving siblings, for whom the inability to communicate about a brother or sister who had died was experienced as an intensely negative—in some cases, the most negative—aspect of the bereavement experience. Thus, it appears that in two areas of working through the bereavement experience, children's and adults' needs are quite different. Another tie-breaking custom—changing residence following a death—was reported, but not frequently enough to be considered a significant coping behavior among respondents.

Table 4–2
Functions of Coping Behaviors

Behavior	Function			
	Acceptance of Loss	Extinction of Nonadaptive Behaviors	Dissipation of Emotions (Anger, Grief, Anxiety)	Maintenance of Continuity and Safety
1. Focusing on school activities			*	*
2. Keeping object of deceased				*
3. Sibling's religious faith			*	
4. Attending services	*			
5. Crying			*	
6. Observing grief of others	*			
7. Engaging in fate-provoking behavior			*	
8. Talking with therapist	*		*	*
9. Writing "dead" on coloring book	*	*	*	
10. Observing parents' faith	*			
11. Looking at picture of deceased			*	*
12. Maintaining normal routine		*		*

Summary

In this chapter we have explored ways in which adults and children cope with loss. Grief and mourning were presented as universal responses to significant loss and the concept of "working-through" loss was reviewed. It was suggested that children use various behaviors in their attempts to cope with loss, including focusing on schoolwork or school-related activities and keeping an object or possession of the deceased. The study findings indicated that children rarely engage in tie-breaking activities (extinction of nonadaptive behavior) but do appear to engage in behaviors which maintain a sense of continuity and safety.

In chapter 5 we will continue to explore coping responses to the loss of a child through excerpts from a taped interview with a family that lost a son nine years ago.

Notes

1. R. Gardner, "Children's Reactions to Parental Death," in *The Child and Death*, ed. J. Schowalter et al. (New York: Columbia University Press, 1983), 104–24.

2. See, for example, M. Wessel, "Children, When Parents Die," in *The Child and Death*, ed. J. Schowalter et al. (New York: Columbia University Press, 1983), 125–34.

3. P. Rosenblatt, R. Walsh, and D. Jackson, *Grief and Mourning in Cross-cultural Perspective* (HRAF Press, 1976), 1.

4. R. Gardner, personal conversation with author.

5. Rosenblatt, Walsh, and Jackson, *Grief and Mourning in Cross-cultural Perspective*, 6.

6. R. Kramer and I. Moore, "Childhood Cancer: Meeting the Special Needs of Healthy Siblings," *Cancer Nursing* (June 1983): 213–17.

7. M. Wessel, "Children, When Parents Die," in *The Child and Death*, ed. J. Schowalter et al. (New York: Columbia University Press, 1983), 127–28.

8. E. Jackson, "The Pastoral Counselor and the Child Encountering Death," in *Helping Children Cope with Death*, ed. H. Wass and C. Carr (Washington, D.C.: Hemisphere Publishing Co., 1982), 33–48.

5
One Family's Story: Interview with the Bakers

> We ought to dance with rapture that we should be alive and in the flesh, and part of the living, incarnate cosmos. I am part of the sun as my eye is part of me. That I am part of the earth my feet know perfectly, and my blood is part of the sea. My soul knows that I am part of the human race . . . as my spirit is part of my nation. In my own very self, I am part of my family.
> — D.H. Lawrence, *Apocalypse*[1]

F amily ties are unlike any other. Members of a family are part of each other in ways that are so subtle, yet so intense, as to be almost beyond description. There is an interconnectedness among the members of a family that is so powerful that it accompanies us throughout all of our days. The influence of our families persists even beyond the time when we have close contact with them; indeed, it may persist even when family members are no longer living.

In viewing the progression of the family, the marriage of a young couple is commonly used as a beginning point. The family life cycle is then traced through the birth of the first child, through the child-rearing years, and through the process of disengagement that takes place as each child—and, finally, the last child—leaves home. This is the expected sequence of events, and it is severely disrupted when a family member dies. Today, especially, when families tend to be smaller, the death of a child exacts a particularly heavy toll. Parents invest so much in each one of their children that the loss of one of them is not easily overcome. Of course, when an only child dies, the loss may be even more difficult to bear.

While most of the research for this book was focused on individual surviving siblings, over time I became more and more aware of the interrelatedness between the siblings' reactions and those of other family members. A picture of childhood sibling loss that did not include a family portrait seemed to be incomplete. Consequently, I began to explore the possibility of meeting with an entire family that had experienced the death of a child. Finding a whole family that was willing to participate in an interview was not a simple task, as there often was one or more family members who did not wish to participate. Through the self-help organization called Compassionate

Friends, I was able eventually to locate a number of families that agreed to talk with me about their experience. The members of one of those families—the Bakers (pseudonym)—were unusually open in their interview and agreed to allow their experience to be retold here.

I met with the Bakers on a sunny winter day at their home in an upper-middle-class community outside Princeton, New Jersey. Mr. and Mrs. Baker are an attractive couple in their early forties. They have three children, Richard, Howard, and Jessica, who are fifteen, twelve, and five years old, respectively. Nine years ago, their firstborn child, Edward, died in a bus accident. My purpose in meeting with the Bakers was to review with them the events of that time—how they coped with their grief and with the changes that ensued in the family as a result of Edward's death. I was particularly interested in how each member of the family had reacted to and coped with the loss, and I wanted to know how the family had changed since then. In the following excerpts from our interviews, the Bakers describe their feelings and actions at the time of the accident and their perspective on the loss today.

> *Dr. Rosen:* I have asked you to sit and talk with me today about what it was like when Edward died and how you as a family coped with that loss. Who would like to begin? Tell me a little bit about what it was like for you? (*Richard points to Mrs. Baker, who then begins.*)
>
> *Mrs. Baker:* Well, we were away vacationing, and the children were home with my mother. It was hard, being so far away, and I think my mother felt extremely guilty because she had the three kids and only returned two . . . and Richard was six and Howard was only three, so they told Richard but they didn't tell Howard, so this meant that I had to tell him when we got back and I felt this was really unfair. But then I understood because I didn't want to tell him either.
>
> *Dr. Rosen:* What happened to Edward?
>
> *Mrs. Baker:* He was on the way home from school and fell under a school bus. . . . It was raining and there were wet leaves and he slipped under the bus. The bus driver saw his hand in the mirror.
>
> *Dr. Rosen (to Richard):* Were you with him at the time?
>
> *Richard:* No, I was at home.
>
> *Howard:* We were waiting for him to go see a movie.
>
> *Dr. Rosen (to Howard):* Do you remember Richard? (*Howard nods.*) What are your memories?
>
> *Howard:* Well, I remember, one morning, well, my dad had these guns that he had on the wall, and he used to take them down and each one of us kids would take a gun and sit with it on Saturday morning and watch T.V. (*Everyone laughs.*)

Dr. Rosen: That's a nice memory. *(Jessica looks sad.)* We're going to get to you, Jessica, don't worry. I have something to ask you too. So, he was the oldest.

Richard and Howard: Yeah.

Mrs. Baker: I worried a lot about that part of it. Richard had been only two years behind in school—they were six and eight—and he followed Edward in everything he did, and I thought it would be real difficult for him without Edward.

Dr. Rosen: Was it, Richard?

Richard: I don't remember.

Dr. Rosen: Were some of his friends your friends also? You know, sometimes when you have an older brother . . .

Richard: Oh, yeah, we had this one kid especially and he was a real good friend and he used to come over all the time. He came over a couple of times after Edward died.

Dr. Rosen: Does he still come over?

Richard: Well, we moved away then.

Dr. Rosen: Do you remember going back to school, Richard, after Edward died?

Richard: I remember the first day. I went back to school and everyone was asking me questions and I ended up leaving, the first day, because it was so traumatic! I don't remember anything after that.

Dr. Rosen: Do you remember what kinds of questions they asked?

Richard: They asked if my brother was dead. . . . All I remember is I walked in the door and was surrounded by a swarm of people. When I walked in, everybody looked up and ran.

Dr. Rosen: Did the teacher say anything, do you remember?

Richard: Um-m . . . no . . . I don't think I was able to hear anything people said anyway.

Dr. Rosen (to Mrs. Baker): Do you remember that, too?

Mrs. Baker: Yeah, he was really uncomfortable and there was a helping mother, she decided that he had had enough so she said to the teacher, "That's enough!" So she took him. I wasn't at home, I was at someone else's house because that was the first day since we buried Edward that I was alone in the house. So she knew where I was and drove him over to my friend's house and she said, "I decided that he'd had enough for one day," and he was fine the next day after that. It was traumatic from the moment he left the house because he took the school bus and when the bus driver opened the door her face was all covered with tears and she said, "You're not going to school today?" and I said, "Yes, he is, and he's going to need your help," and when I got back in the house I realized that this same woman had been on that bus when Edward died.

The preceding excerpt illustrates the way in which school personnel, through interactions with the bereaved family, can convey their attitudes and expectations regarding a child's loss. In this case, the school's perception of when the surviving sibling should return to school differed from the family's view. Both the helping mother and the school bus driver expressed the view that it was "too soon" for Richard to be back in school. Clearly, these were members of the bereaved community who had been saddened by Edward's death. The surviving sibling's return to school elicited a protective response toward him and was painful for *them* as well.

Dr. Rosen: It was pretty soon after that you all got back. (*To Mr. Baker.*) You went back to work then, too? (*Mr. Baker nods.*) Was that difficult for you, or helpful?

Mr. Baker: Yes, both.

Dr. Rosen (to Mrs. Baker): And what did you do?

Mrs. Baker (nodding at Howard): Well, he was just three, so I was busy with him.

Mr. Baker: She wrote a book!

Mrs. Baker: Well, I needed to do something. When everybody went back to school and work I felt really cheated! That I was the only one who was left in the house. There was Edward's chair, and I was the one to move the chair away from the table. There was the physical aspect of the house—someone had to do it.

Dr. Rosen: What did you do with his things? What kinds of changes did you make?

Mrs. Baker: The first thing was moving the chair back and actually it was better for the balance at the table. There had been five chairs and now there was an even four. All three kids had been in the same room and Richard and Edward shared a bunk bed, so Richard moved to the top.

Richard: I don't remember there being a bunk bed at all, but if there was, I was always on the top.

Mrs. Baker: Oh yes, there was!

Mrs. Baker: And he [Howard] also took the blanket that was Edward's. It was his favorite thing. Then later we divided all of Edward's possessions up.

Dr. Rosen: Who was "we"—who was that?

Mrs. Baker: The whole family.

Dr. Rosen: The whole family sat down together.

Mrs. Baker: All of Edward's clothes I put away in a box . . . and about six months later I pulled the box out, and I discovered, which I really had known, at the time, it was fall when Edward died, and all the clothes still had the store tags on them and, so this was like, a difficult time for me. Anything that he had worn was already cycled through the kids by this time, so we didn't even think, somehow . . . I always thought of those particular clothes that had been in the dresser at that time as the ones that were really Edward's clothes.

Dr. Rosen (to Richard and Howard): Did either of you ask to keep anything of Edward's?

Mrs. Baker: All the kids took possessions. We let them choose.

Howard: Except the kite. We had this kite that they bought for him. They kept it.

Mrs. Baker: Yeah, we had this kite that we bought on vacation. It was supposed to be for the three kids but it was really his. He always dictated everything . . . so we never could give it to the kids. . . . So it took seven years and on what would have been his sixteenth birthday, we each took a turn flying the kite.

Richard: Not me.

Mrs. Baker: You weren't home. He was away, but he knew what we were doing. Then we let go and watched it disappear. But the other things we kept.

Dr. Rosen: And you have them put away somewhere?

Mrs. Baker: Yes . . . and, of course, there are pictures.

Dr. Rosen: I was just going to ask about that.

Mrs. Baker: In fact, in the dining area we have a family tree, sort of. There's only one picture of Edward by himself, one picture of the three boys, another of the two boys with Jessica.

Dr. Rosen: You're a very different family now than you were back then. Let me ask you one other thing. At the funeral service for Edward—you mentioned the viewing—did Howard and Richard go?

Mrs. Baker: (*Howard and Richard shake their heads no.*) They were invited but they didn't go.

Dr. Rosen: They chose not to? (*To Howard and Richard.*) Do either of you have any memory of that? Of why you chose not to go?

Richard: I just didn't want to go.

Howard: I think I chose not to go because he chose not to.

Dr. Rosen: That makes sense. So where did they stay? Did someone come and stay with them?

Mrs. Baker: They stayed at the house. Someone stayed with them— several people stayed with them because we were afraid that with a death, especially the death of a child that's front-page news . . . it's not safe.

The children's decision not to attend the viewing of the brother was not atypical, although some children do prefer to accompany parents to all funeral services and may even feel left out if they are prohibited from attending. Generally, children over the age of four or five can make this decision for themselves and, of course, should have their wishes respected in this regard.

Dr. Rosen (to Mrs. Baker): You told me before that you had to tell Howard. Richard already knew because his grandmother told him.

Mrs. Baker: Yes, but apparently he got the idea that Edward had a broken leg, and when my mother told him he got very upset and said, "I knew it wasn't just a broken leg."

Richard: Yeah, I remember that.

Mrs. Baker: And when I told Howard, Howard said "No, he's okay. He's just in the hospital, he has a broken leg." I don't know where he got that. In fact, I think his arm was broken.

Dr. Rosen (to parents): You were away, so you found out by your mother calling you?

Mrs. Baker: We were in California. It took us six hours to fly back, the worst plane ride of my life. A bad plane ride (*some laughter*). Well, Dad doesn't fly well, that made it worse.

Mr. Baker: I'm like the pope, I kiss the ground when I get off the plane!

Dr. Rosen: I'm with you. I must admit, it's hard for me to fly also. (*To Mr. and Mrs. Baker.*) How much do you remember about—did you talk much about all of this, share what you felt with one another?

Mrs. Baker: Despite his reticence here today, yes, we did.

Dr. Rosen: You're saying he talked a lot more than he is now? (*Laughter.*)

Mrs. Baker: Well, you can see he's a very quiet and private person. So most of the talking was from me—one-sided—but when he said things they seemed to mean so much more. I would take a whole day to say the same thing.

Dr. Rosen (to Mr. and Mrs. Baker): What about the two of you and the boys? Do you remember sitting around ever and talking about what had happened?

Richard: No. All I remember is when we had a paper boy who was a real tall big boy who had seen the accident and he had been in and you two had been talking. And that's all I remember about talking, except when we had all the cousins over and the whole house was full of kids and you two were always talking, but I was playing.

Mrs. Baker: We did talk a little bit. He [Richard] didn't cry at the time. But about ten months later, my sister had this dog that she wanted to give to us, and I said no, and he cried and cried and cried. And I said to my sister, "He's not crying about the dog," but that's the way he was, he had to have what he felt was an acceptable excuse.

Dr. Rosen: Who cried the most?

Mrs. Baker: I guess me. (*Mr. Baker nods agreement.*)

Mrs. Baker (indicating both boys): They did their grieving in their sleep.

Dr. Rosen: Bad dreams? Nightmares?

Mrs. Baker: He [Richard] had nightmares, not nightmares that would wake him up but if the lights went out, he would call out, and Howard wet the bed.

Howard (laughing): I was good at it.

Dr. Rosen (to Mr. Baker): Did you ever cry? (*Mr. Baker shakes his head no.*)

Mrs. Baker: Yes, you did. You cried with me.

Dr. Rosen: The two of you cried together? (*They nod.*)

Like many of the fathers alluded to in previous chapters, Mr. Baker was less verbal about his feelings of loss than his wife. In fact, he was quite friendly and conversed freely about many topics *after* the interview was officially over. Clearly, the experience of bereavement caused him to be uncharacteristically reserved.

Dr. Rosen: Do you have a lot of family around, you know, aunts, uncles, cousins?

Mr. Baker: Well, Grandma . . .

Mrs. Baker: My mother. I have a sister and we see her maybe a couple of times a year.

Dr. Rosen: When Edward died, were there a lot of people who came to the house?

Richard: The house was packed.

Mrs. Baker: There were so many people, from church and from Edward's school, and they all brought food! I remember taking Richard aside and saying, "You know the miracle of five feeding five thousand? Well, we had five thousand feeding five," and it was a bit much.

Dr. Rosen: Was it helpful to have people come?

Mrs. Baker: It helped a lot. The problem was it stopped. One friend came over about six months later and I answered the door and she said, "Here, I had saved this spaghetti dinner for six months and I thought this might be a day you could use it," and she was right, I really could use it then.

Like many bereaved families, the Bakers experienced the power of the taboo on speaking the name of the deceased, particularly in relation to non-family others. In this next excerpt, they discuss this problem as well as means they began to use to emerge from their grief.

Dr. Rosen (to Richard): Do you remember anything that people said to you—did the neighbors, relatives, say anything to you that you remember?

Richard: No. They tried not to talk to us. I don't know why.

Mrs. Baker: I think he's right. They really did avoid talking to them. I think they were afraid that the kids would cry. They were that way with us, too. They would always say, "Would it upset you if I talked about this?" What they meant was, "You will upset me if I talk about this, so let's not!" We discussed this afterwards—it was like a big barrier between us—we had to comfort our friends rather than the other way around. It was almost that you had to rush into this topic and get that part over with and then you could be friendly again. It was the reverse of what I thought it would be like. We were more comfortable talking about it because we had to handle it on a day-to-day basis.

Dr. Rosen: What do you remember doing, each one of you, that made you feel better? Can you remember any kinds of activities or things that you did that helped you during this time?

Mrs. Baker: Church was helpful. Some reading was helpful—I didn't read about grief at the time, but since then. Edward was dyslexic and I spent a lot of time in the library reading all I could about dyslexia. But then I decided that since the kids were so little, I was afraid they wouldn't remember, so I sat down and wrote Edward's life story. And as I would write it I would give it to him [Mr. Baker] to read. And the two of us—I think I kind of did my grieving through writing it and he did it through reading it. Another thing we did was to have some sharing time each day.

Dr. Rosen: Who was involved with that?

Mrs. Baker: The whole family.

Richard (to Mrs. Baker): But you were the leader.

Mrs. Baker: Well, yeah. There always has to be a leader.

Dr. Rosen: What about you, Richard? Do you remember anything that made you feel better?

Richard: No.

Mrs. Baker: I remember something, Richard. You were getting undressed one day—it was about a year after—and suddenly out of the blue he says that you know, since Edward was dead, some things were better. I said, "*Like what?*" but he couldn't identify it. Just some things were better. A few months after that he came in so excited from playing and said, "It's just like before Edward died." What had happened was that all the children on the block who used to gather at our house and had stopped coming over, on that day they had all come back and he was *so* pleased. . . . We did do some other things. We decided at one point that we wanted to make some changes. We moved, and of course, we had Jessica (after a disastrous experience with a foster child and we decided that we did not want to do that). I think that in making that decision things really began to get better.

Dr. Rosen: When was that?

Mrs. Baker: We made that decision about a year and a half after we finally moved into the house, and had the baby about three years later.

Dr. Rosen: Did you all want to move?

Richard: I don't think that I wanted to move.

Howard: I wanted to move because at that time I didn't have any friends nearby. There was a house next door and I went there sometimes. I had about three friends and they had all moved away. I just decided I didn't want to stay there. I didn't have any friends.

Dr. Rosen: Richard, do you remember why you didn't want to move?

Mrs. Baker: He had a lot of friends.

In this next portion of the interview, the Bakers talk about how their family has changed since Edward's death nine years ago. In particular, they describe how Richard assumed, to some degree, the leadership role of the oldest child, and how the family's priorities have been reordered.

Dr. Rosen: In some ways your family is obviously different now than it was before Edward's death. Jessica is one example—right, Jessica? You're part of this family now. Do any of you have any impressions of other ways in which the family has changed?

Howard: Yeah, sports!

Richard: Yeah—Edward, he hated sports because he couldn't do them. So, I didn't do them and Howard didn't do them. But now, after he died, I've been getting a lot more into football and baseball and wrestling. I've been getting into that more—and Howard runs and shoots.

Mr. Baker: Edward generally decided what we did as a family. If he was interested in something, we all did it. He sort of dictated what we as a family did together. We were always going to things that interested Edward.

Dr. Rosen: Has anyone else in the family assumed the position that Edward had as the dominant one?

Everyone (laughing): Richard!

Mrs. Baker: I think it's kind of a natural role for the oldest child. Parents aren't taught how to be parents; it's always experimentation. In our family, we always look to the oldest child for direction. And if he likes wrestling, then you become a wrestling family.

Richard: Even Jessica follows me!

Mrs. Baker: That's true. Jessica now plays heavy metal rock in her room!

Dr. Rosen: Are there any other ways that you as a family have changed?

Mrs. Baker: I think we are a much closer family now. Our priorities have definitely changed. It wasn't really that they were wrong. The church was always a part of our lives, and it still is. But the family is more important to us now. We worry more about each other, rather than other people.

Dr. Rosen: So what happens to each one of you is more important than what happens outside of the family.

Mrs. Baker: Exactly.

Dr. Rosen: Well, Jessica, you didn't know Edward. Do you look at the pictures of him sometimes? (*She nods.*) What do you think about all this sitting around and talking about Edward? Do you want to say anything about it?

Jessica: I feel left out, because I didn't know him.

Dr. Rosen: So when the family talks about Edward, you feel left out. (*She nods.*)

Dr. Rosen: Well, how do you all feel today about it?

Mrs. Baker: It's not an experience I'd ever want to repeat.

Dr. Rosen: Do you ever worry about its happening to another child?

Mrs. Baker: Of course. It's the greatest fear a parent can have, and it's a greater fear than when your family is intact.

Dr. Rosen: Do you think it affects your behavior as parents, that you're overprotective of the kids because of it?

Mrs. Baker: The kids would say so. I don't think we are.

Richard: Yes, you are, come on.

Howard: Be serious, Mom!

Mrs. Baker: In fact, at times I go to the opposite extreme, let them do things that I shouldn't. One time, Richard wanted to ride his bike to the mall. He was just a little guy and not that good on his bike yet and I let him. And when he got there, he called me and said "I made it, and you were right, I shouldn't have ridden to the mall!"

Finally, in this last excerpt, Mrs. Baker describes so-called fate-provoking behavior on Richard's part as he neared the age of Edward at his death.

Dr. Rosen: Is there anything else anyone wants to say that we haven't covered? I don't necessarily have all the best questions.

Mrs. Baker: One thing that happened—when Richard got to be the same age as Edward was when he died, he really started acting bizarre. It was as if he was challenging fate! He went off and climbed a mountain all by himself, and he ran away.

Richard: Oh, come on. We had already climbed that mountain that day.

Dr. Rosen: Did he get down by himself?

Mrs. Baker: He did, but we were very concerned. We had called the police.

Dr. Rosen: Was there any discussion that Richard was now the age that Edward had been?

Mrs. Baker: Well, every year on his birthday we would mention that Edward would have been so many years old, and I had heard the boys talking about it themselves. So just to get it out of the way, when Richard got to be one day older than Edward had been, I said to him, "You're the oldest child I ever had," and things seemed to settle down after that.

The reader can, I think, appreciate the experience of the Baker family in a variety of ways. The discomfort of neighbors and friends in making their condolence calls juxtaposed to their generous donations of food and their very presence is typical in our society. The difficult return to normal life following the death, the need to cope with anniversaries, the fear of another tragedy occurring—these issues have been described by numerous individuals who have experienced the death of a significant family member. The Baker family also demonstrates remarkable resilience and the ability to adapt: a new child was born, not as a replacement for the son who died, but, at least in part, as an affirmation that the family is still alive. Roles were rearranged and priorities reordered. The family has not forgotten Edward, but it can laugh again. In some ways, the family members feel even closer now than they did before the loss.

In chapter 6 we will focus on sibling and family styles of coping with a somewhat different circumstance—cancer in a young child. Living with a life-threatening illness poses some unique problems in addition to the many we have already discussed.

Note

1. D.H. Lawrence, "Apocalypse," in *Apocalypse and the Writings on Revelation*, ed. M. Kalnins (Cambridge: Cambridge University Press, 1980), 149, reprinted with permission.

6
Living with a Dying Sibling

When my sister died, I felt somewhat relieved that the ordeal was over for her and for the rest of the family. She had been sick with leukemia for three years prior to her death and was very sick the last month or so. It was difficult watching her suffer over those years and because we were so close in age I felt somewhat like the protector. Other children used to make fun of her because of the side effects of chemotherapy, and I was very upset by this and always afraid someone would tell her she had leukemia since she did not know (supposedly—I think she did).

— surviving sibling

The long and drawn-out suffering of a child and brother is tragic and wearying.

— surviving sibling

About two thousand new cases of childhood cancer are identified each year. Advances in treatment during the past ten to fifteen years have been astonishing, and the diagnosis today of cancer in childhood is not invariably a death sentence. Still, childhood cancer is the leading cause of death from disease in children under fifteen years of age.[1] Children also die of other life-threatening illnesses, including kidney disorders, cystic fibrosis, and lupus. Whatever the circumstances, "There is no more devastating experience in the life of a family than the fatal illness and death of a child."[2] It destroys the normal functioning of the family unit and presents each member of the family with a personal crisis.

Coping with Life-threatening Illness

Children who have life-threatening or terminal illnesses must cope with the specter of impending death as well as all the social implications of living with a severe and debilitating disease.[3] In the case of terminal illness, it is highly probable that individuals who are close to or around the dying child will attempt to shield the child from the knowledge that his or her situation is critical. Despite their good intentions, efforts of this kind will probably increase the child's sense of isolation and anxiety rather than allay it.[4] On the other hand, treating the child with candor—without dispelling hope—has been demonstrated to be effective and useful to the emotional adjustment of the child.[5] The evidence is not yet overwhelming, though, in favor of open communication, and some still favor the protective approach toward the child with terminal illness.[6]

Siblings of Critically Ill Children

It is clear that brothers and sisters of children with cancer and other life-threatening conditions experience a variety of problems resulting from the tragic circumstances of their lives. Failure to thrive, for example, is more common among very young siblings of pediatric cancer patients,[7] and siblings of chronically ill children tend to be more withdrawn and irritable than are siblings of healthy children.[8] As one might expect, the impact of living with a dying sibling depends to some degree on the developmental level of the well sibling.[9] But there is an ironic aspect to siblings' unique position in the family: not only do they fare the worst when the patient is in greatest pain; they often do poorly even when others in the family are doing relatively well. John Spinetta writes:

> The siblings seem to lose out on both ends. . . . When the patient is doing poorly, parental attention is focused on helping the patient through that particular crisis and the siblings are left without attention and needed support. When the patient is again doing well, parental concerns shift to other non-disease-related matters and the siblings are again left without support.[10]

The impact of living with a seriously ill sibling is not always negative. Some siblings experience little effect and tend to minimize the experience,[11] while in other families the experience may actually promote positive caring between the siblings and parents.[12] Siblings who live with a critically ill sister or brother may also acquire a greater understanding of other children with special problems, as well as an ability to handle a greater degree of responsibility.[13] Still, less is known about the ways in which children cope with the presence of a terminally ill sibling than about the psychopathology and disturbance that may result from this circumstance.

With regard to communication in the family concerning a critically ill child, the most important factor in determining the siblings' reactions may be "the honesty and appropriateness with which the parents communicate with them about the ill child and the nature of the problem."[14] But in general, most parents elect not to inform the siblings that the disease is terminal, in the mistaken belief that "they wouldn't understand" or "we thought it better not to burden them."[15]

Siblings of Children with Cancer

The survey of adult survivors of sibling loss revealed forty seven reports of sibling death due to illness of more than two months' duration and with prior awareness (or suspicion) of impending death. Nineteen of these deaths were due to cancer—primarily leukemia—with the remainder resulting from heart disease or birth defect in the heart, polio, lupus, kidney disorders, or cystic fibrosis. More direct information was obtained from working directly with siblings of pediatric cancer patients. This work was conducted in the Department of Pediatrics at Cooper Hospital/University Medical Center in Camden, New Jersey, in conjunction with the Division of Hematology/Oncology (Dr. Milton H. Donaldson, Head, Debbie Feierman, M.S.W., Social Worker), and involved both psychological testing of siblings of pediatric patients and the development and implementation of a support group for the healthy siblings. Seven boys between the ages of nine and twelve participated in the program, although only six were tested. The psychological testing measured the well sibling's preoccupation with threat (fear of death) through the administration of a projective test developed by Eugenia Waechter for her study of terminally ill children.[16] Test scores were also obtained from a control group of children who were comparable in age, ethnicity, sex, and geographic location but who had well siblings. These children were students at a local elementary school in southern New Jersey.

The Projective Test

The projective test developed by Eugenia Waechter consists of a set of eight pictures. Four of the pictures were taken from the standard Thematic Apperception Test (TAT)[17] and four were specifically designed for her study of death anxiety in children who have fatal illness (see Appendix E). The rationale behind this kind of test is that if an individual is asked to create a story describing what is happening in a picture, the story that is created will be a reflection of his or her own needs, concerns, and worries. Pictures are made intentionally vague so as to offer a minimum of cues that might influence the storyteller. The four pictures designed expressly for Waechter's study depict children in bed or in the hospital.

Table 6–1 presents situational information on the six boys who participated in the program of testing, including their age, the sibling's age, the sibling's diagnosis, and the time elapsed since the initial diagnosis. All of the diagnosed siblings were in good condition (remission) during the time of the testing, and all were male except for the sister of sibling number B3.

Table 6–1
Situational Information on Boys and Their Siblings

Child Number	Age	Sibling's Age	Sibling's Diagnosis	Time Since Diagnosis
B1	11	10	Acute lymphocytic leukemia	3 months
B2	11	18	Brain tumor	5 months
B3	10	5	Acute lymphocytic leukemia	11 months
B4	12	11	Acute lymphocytic leukemia	2½ years
B5	11	9	Acute lymphocytic leukemia	1 month
B6	9	4	Acute lymphocytic leukemia	6 months

Fear of Death in Siblings of Children with Cancer

Eugenia Waechter's hypothesis was that the fear of death, while not expressed directly and openly by many fatally ill children, may nevertheless be present. The projective test with pictures was utilized to elicit indirect expression of that anxiety. Further, Waechter postulated that:

> The fear of death from inside the body may be denied but exteriorized and displaced to threat from without . . . so that the environment itself appears to be menacing. Fear of separation or loneliness and fear of mutilation, intrusive procedures and pain may substitute for an underlying general apprehensiveness about survival. . . . These fears and others may be an outcropping, or objective way of expressing an underlying anxiety.[18]

Consequently, the projective test used to measure these fears is scored both in terms of total fear and specific themes related to death anxiety. In reviewing the results of this test, we will examine the total fear score and the three subcategories of loneliness/separation, mutilation, and death anxiety. The purpose of this research activity was to provide additional documentation on siblings of children with cancer to show that they *are* seriously affected by the illness, as well as to shed more light on the specific concerns that become the focus of the well sibling's anxiety and to delineate more clearly how that anxiety may be expressed.

Table 6–2 shows both the range of scores and the average scores of six groups of children. The first four groups included children with fatal illness, those with chronic illness but a good prognosis, those with brief illness, and healthy (nonhospitalized) children. Scores for these groups were obtained by Waechter. Children within this sample were matched for age, race, social class, and length of hospitalization. Because of the small number of siblings

Table 6–2
Total Fear Scores

Group	Range of Scores	Average Score
Fatal	3–65	53.31
Chronic (good prognosis)	5–36	17.75
Brief	8–29	18.19
Normal (Waechter)	– 1–29	11.06
Normal (Rosen)	20–40	27.04
Siblings	31–41	36.16

Source: Adapted from E. Waechter, "Death Anxiety in Children with Fatal Illness," Ph.D. diss., Stanford University, 1968.

available for our study in this book, no matching with Waechter's sample was possible. It should be noted that the group of siblings, ranging in age from nine to twelve, was somewhat older than the children in Waechter's sample, who were between the ages of six and ten. An additional "normal" group was sampled in order to offer a truer comparison to the sibling group. This sample, which is listed as "Normal (Rosen)" on the table, consisted of nine children comparable to the siblings of children with cancer in terms of age, sex (all boys), socioeconomic status, ethnicity, and location of residence.

The sibling group scored in the range of 31 to 41 on total fear relation motivation, with an average score of 36.16, which represents the combined scores of all categories scored for each child. These scores indicate that levels of generalized death anxiety were higher for the siblings of children with cancer than for the nonhospitalized children or the children with brief or chronic (good prognosis) illness. Children with fatal illness scored the highest, with an average score of 53.31.

Table 6–3 shows scores for the same groups in three imagery subcategories: loneliness/separation, mutilation, and death. Within the subcategory of mutilation, all six groups scored in the same range, so there was no statistical significance. With regard to death imagery, though, the sibling group scored markedly higher than either the normal (nonhospitalized) groups or the briefly and chronically ill (good prognosis) groups, and almost as high as the fatally ill children. *The sibling group scored highest* in the loneliness/ separation subcategory—even markedly above the fatally ill children.

For example, one twelve-year-old boy whose brother had been diagnosed two and one half years earlier with A.L.L. (child number B4 on table 6–1) told the following story after viewing picture card H, which depicts a small child sitting in the doorway of a cabin (TAT 13B):

Table 6–3
Imagery Scores

Group	Average Percentage of Subjects' Use of Imagery in Scorable Stories		
	Loneliness/Separation	Mutilation	Death
Fatal	27.73	54.62	63.03
Chronic (good prognosis)	6.76	35.13	17.57
Brief	6.76	35.13	17.57
Normal (Waechter)	1.64	44.26	6.56
Normal (Rosen)	12.20	37.00	16.00
Siblings	43.75	39.58	60.00

Source: Adapted from E. Waechter, "Death Anxiety in Children with Fatal Illness," Ph.D. diss., Stanford University, 1968.

> The boy is lonely. It might be an old house that nobody lives in anymore. He walked in and looked around. It might be his house, burned down. He's thinking he's going to use it as a clubhouse and live in it so he can live old memories.

Another child (number B2) told the following story from the same card:

> He probably doesn't have anyone to play with. It's a farm and there's hardly anyone to play with. It's a wooden house and he has no shoes—maybe it's hot. He wants to move from there because hardly any friends come around. Either he'll move or some people will move there so he has friends to play with.

In contrast, a child from the comparison group of well siblings, listed as "Normal (Rosen)" on tables 6–2 and 6–3, told the following story:

> A little boy is in a barn or log cabin. It's dark inside. He must have something big on his mind. He's nervous—thinking something over—he wants to be alone. He'll think until he finds a solution and then go to his parents and talk to them about it.

Mutilation imagery in stories told by siblings of cancer patients often revolves around medical procedures. One nine-year-old boy (child number B6) was preoccupied in many of his stories with the procedures his brother had undergone. He told this story after viewing card B, which was designed for Waechter's study and depicts a small child in a hallway outside a closed door leading to the ICU:

The girl looks like she broke her arm. She's going into ICU. Her mother's right behind her. When she goes in, she gets treatment and everything and she feels awful, all doped up like my brother.

In response to card A showing two boys in adjoining beds, child number B1 related:

Both boys have leukemia, are in the hospital to be treated. They want their families to stay. They will be treated with needles (which they don't want) and have to drink a lot of juice, water and other liquids.

Finally, a number of stories were related on the subject of death imagery. For instance, in response to card F, which shows a child in bed, with parents and a doctor outside the door, an eleven-year-old boy (child number B2) said:

The girl is probably dying. The doctor is talking to her mother and father. The mother and father are asking how she is doing and the doctor says she's doing well. They'll ask to see her and she'll start talking to them. She'll either get well or she might die.

Styles of Coping in the Family

As noted earlier in this chapter, the presence of a critically ill child in a family leads to unintentional "neglect" of the healthy siblings and to a lack of communication between them and their parents. It is important to point out that the same factors were observed in the families of these children with cancer. For instance, one family reported that in between periods when medical complications absorbed their energies, much of their attention was focused on reestablishing an equilibrium, that is, on living a normal life. Another family reported that as the ill child's symptoms waned (went into remission), normal interaction among family members was strongly emphasized. Most families reported that although the well sibling was informed of the ill child's disease and need for treatment, there was little discussion of the potentially serious consequences of the disease. Nevertheless, some siblings sensed this possibility from the responses of the other family members.

The Sibling Support Group

The sibling support group met at Cooper Hospital/University Medical Center in New Jersey and was organized to meet some of the needs of the siblings of pediatric cancer patients. Debbie Feierman, a pediatric social worker, was the group leader and met with seven boys aged nine to twelve for two and one half hours every other week. The group met in a playroom equipped with toys, games, and medical supplies. The room was also supplied with a two-way mirror for observation by the author and the child life specialist, Judy Strassman. The group met over a period of five months (it was terminated when the approach of spring brought many competing activities into the children's lives), and during this time, it was possible to observe both deep concerns and attempts at coping in the siblings who attended each meeting. Themes of mutilation and death predominated in much of the boys' play. Humor, identification with the aggressor, and denial were observed as adaptive and defensive measures. In fact, the boys openly expressed many concerns similar to those revealed by their stories. Needles and medical procedures formed the core of these concerns:

> During the first two sessions, medical syringes were used by the boys as squirt guns. When Aaron arrived for session 3, he filled a syringe and began squirting into the air. Bob said, "My brother gets four needles every day." Then he looked through an otoscope. Carl filled a second syringe and challenged Aaron but Aaron put down his syringe, saying, "I'm out of needle fight." Donald took the syringe, filled it and threatened to shoot the others. After a few more minutes of play Donald said to Aaron, "Prepare to die."[19]

And at a later session:

> Donald and Aaron examined the otoscope and stethoscope. Donald said, "I can't hear your heart." Aaron said, "Oh, no, I'm dead." Aaron commented about syringes, "I don't like them," and later, "Anybody want a needle?"[20]

The use of humor to veil anxieties about death and mutilation was observed in the sixth meeting, when the boys decided to "perform surgery" on the group leader:

> Carl and Aaron, gowned, masked and gloved, with medical equipment prepared, told the patient (group leader), "This'll be just like 'M*A*S*H.' You're gonna die." A "petrified" reply only got the "patient" a shove to lie down on the operating table. She was told, "This isn't gonna hurt ... and you'll get a lollipop when you're finished." "Drs." Carl and Aaron got the IV [intravenous] flowing, pulled out all the pretend knives and needles. When the group leader asked if she would die from this, Aaron assured her, "You'll come out of this if you cooperate." While carefully examining the operating tools, Carl was quickly summoned by Aaron for his assistance. "She's bleeding," Carl replied rather matter-of-factly. "Either make her better or let her bleed to death." With no success in making the patient better, the "doctors" left the group leader on the table to die. Aaron said, "Having an

operation, you wonder if you'll ever come out of it." Carl consoled Aaron. "We can relax now, we've killed another patient." They shook hands, "Nice job, Doctor. Let's go to the coffin room."[21]

The boys were able to deal with their feelings quite directly at times. During play, when hospital IV equipment was being used, for example, the following exchange developed:

Craig commented that he had IV medications following an operation when he was younger. Frank replied that his sister has gotten IV medications too. Donald asked, with some evidence of anxiety, if there would be patients coming to the offices today, to which he received a negative reply. Carl then asked if his sister used this playroom when she comes to see the doctor. He was satisfied to have the examining room pointed out with the explanation that "patients are seen there by the nurse and/or doctor and medical procedures are done in those examining rooms." Carl replied, "Yeah, Susie sees Dr. Jones there." Donald questioned why Carl's sister saw Dr. Jones, to which Carl replied, "She has leukemia." Donald indicated that he, too, has a brother [David] who sees Dr. Jones and added, "I'm glad I'm not David." When the group leader asked him why, Donald responded sadly, "Because he has leukemia." "Leukemia is a very serious disease that requires lots of treatment," replied the group leader. "Yeah," said Donald, "you gotta get shots and stuff." Despite his previous knowledge about this group, Donald asked, "Does everyone in here have a brother or sister with leukemia?" Carl readily shared that he has a sister with leukemia and, slowly, the other members shared the experience of their siblings' disease. Carl explained that his sister "lost her hair" and revealed how that was handled rather humorously by his sister and their family. Donald said, "I thought David was gonna turn into a monster and look real gross when he lost his hair." The group leader reflected on how scary it is: "You don't know what they're gonna look like bald." Carl quickly assured the group that "it's 'cause of the chemotherapy but it grows back. My sister's hair has grown back nice now!" Frank commented on how his brother's hair has grown back "straighter than before," and Donald offers that "David's is just beginning to come in."[22]

The sibling support group was offered as one part of a comprehensive treatment approach whose aim was to provide care to the entire family involved with pediatric cancer. Optimally, any program for treating the psychosocial needs of the siblings of terminally ill children would include opportunity for peer-group contact along with other treatment modalities. Meeting with others who have an ill brother or sister provides the healthy sibling with an opportunity that is invaluable and impossible to duplicate— the experience of being with others who are "in the same boat" and who understand, perhaps better than anyone, what it is like to be the sibling of a terminally ill child.

Summary

One of the siblings of a pediatric cancer patient told the following story about the child depicted in card B:

> She's frustrated, angry, mad, happy, and sad. Frustrated because somebody is in the hospital. Angry because she can't see them. Happy because she knows they'll be feeling better after the operation—crying, because she's sad.

Clearly, having a sister or brother diagnosed and under treatment for childhood cancer is an ordeal for healthy siblings that elicits the widest possible range of emotions and concerns. Well siblings worry about whether their sister or brother will get better, whether the illness is contagious, whether their own needs will still be met in the family. They are also intensely affected by the treatment routines that permeate their siblings' lives. The healthy siblings studied here specifically demonstrated deep concern about whether their siblings would live or die and revealed fear of and preoccupation with needles and other related medical procedures and the physical changes observed in their siblings as a result of treatment. They also indicated through their responses to the projective test that they felt lonely and isolated. These findings suggest that programs for children who have siblings with terminal or life-threatening illnesses need to have three primary goals:

1. *Education*—helping the siblings to understand and appreciate the nature of their brother's or sister's illness and the treatment procedures involved

2. *Reduction of isolation and provision of support*—establishing an environment in which siblings can feel their own needs being acknowledged and met, in which caring adults can provide support for their efforts to cope, and in which peer contact can be established

3. *Ventilation*—providing an opportunity for siblings to communicate their feelings, concerns, and questions about their brothers' and sisters' illnesses and any related issues

Programs designed with these goals in mind will have the capacity to offer extensive assistance to siblings of seriously ill children. In addition, they will greatly aid the family that is struggling to cope with the threatened loss of one of its members. Indeed, the programs will be most effective when included as part of an overall plan that takes into consideration and treats all members of the family living with childhood cancer.

Notes

1. F. Kung, "From Diagnosis to Survival," in *Living with Childhood Cancer* (St. Louis: C.V. Mosby, 1981), 81–85.

2. J.M. Weiner, "Reactions of the Family to the Fatal Illness of a Child," in *Loss and Grief: Psychological Management in Medical Practice* (New York: Columbia University Press, 1970), 87.

3. See, for example, M. Bluebond-Langner, *The Private Worlds of Dying Children* (Princeton, New Jersey: Princeton University Press, 1978).

4. E. Waechter, "Children's Awareness of Fatal Illness," *American Journal of Nursing* 71, no. 6 (1971) 1168–72.

5. J. Vernick and M. Karon, "Who's Afraid of Death on a Leukemia Ward?" *American Journal of Diseases of Children* 109 (1965): 393–97.

6. R. Share, "Family Communication in the Crises of a Child's Fatal Illness: Literature Review and Analysis," *OMEGA: Journal of Death and Dying* 3, no. 30 (1972): 187–201.

7. S. Lansky, L. Stephenson, E. Weller, G. Cavins, Jr., and N. Cavins, "Failure to Thrive During Infancy in Siblings of Pediatric Cancer Patients," *American Journal of Pediatric Hematology/Oncology* 4, no. 4 (1982): 361–66.

8. J. Lavigne and M. Ryan, "Psychological Adjustments of Siblings of Children with Chronic Illness," *Pediatrics* 63, no. 4 (1979): 616–27.

9. M. Lindsay and D. MacCarthy, "Caring for the Brothers and Sisters of a Dying Child," in *Care of the Child Facing Death,* ed. L. Burton (London: Routledge and Kegan Paul, 1974), 189–206.

10. J. Spinetta, "The Sibling of the Child with Cancer," in *Living with Childhood Cancer* (St. Louis: C.V. Mosby, 1981), 140.

11. J. Gogan, G. Koocher, D. Foster, and J. O'Malley, "Impact of Childhood Cancer on Siblings," *Health and Social Work* 2 no. 1 (1977): 42–57.

12. B. Sourkes, "Siblings of the Pediatric Cancer Patient," in *Psychological Aspects of Childhood Cancer,* ed. J. Kellerman (Springfield, Ill.: Charles C. Thomas, 1981), 26.

13. Lavigne and Ryan, "Psychological Adjustments of Siblings of Children with Chronic Illness."

14. Weiner, "Reactions of the Family to the Fatal Illness of a Child," 96.

15. J. Stebbens and A. Lascari, "Psychological Follow-up of Families with Childhood Leukemia," *Journal Clinical Psychology* 30 (1974): 394–97.

16. E. Waechter, "Death Anxiety in Children with Fatal Illness," Ph.D. diss., Stanford University, 1968.

17. H. Murray, *Thematic Apperception Test* (Cambridge, Mass.: Harvard University Press, 1943).

18. Waechter, "Death Anxiety in Children with Fatal Illness," 20–21.

19. H. Rosen, D. Feierman, and J. Strassman, "Group Therapy for Siblings of Children with Cancer," unpublished paper, 12.

20. Ibid.

21. Ibid., 13.

22. Ibid.

7
Surviving Sibling Loss

Perhaps the most difficult factor to evaluate regarding sibling death in childhood is the long-range impact of the loss. What, if any, are the consequences of sibling loss on the development of a child? How does grieving or failure to grieve in childhood influence the adult personality? Are survivors of sibling loss at greater risk of developing emotional disorders or any predictable type of conflict in later years? These are obviously questions of great interest and importance for anyone concerned with the study of childhood bereavement. They are also questions that pose highly complex methodological problems.[1]

In looking at the long-term effects of childhood bereavement, observers have again tended to focus primarily on parental loss, relegating the investigation of sibling loss once more to the back burner. In the few exceptions to this trend, observers have examined the relationship between parental and sibling loss in childhood and subsequent rates of schizophrenia;[2] the relationship between sibling loss and adult creativity;[3] and depression, suicide, and psychosis as they occur during anniversary periods of earlier sibling death.[4] Evidence exists that indicates a relationship between parental loss in childhood and subsequent development of emotional disorders,[5] but overall, the data are still inconclusive. We cannot offer definitive answers with regard to the long-range effects of sibling loss either, but some of the issues that such a loss might pose for adult survivors were identified in the form of three content areas: (1) characteristics of interpersonal behavior, (2) death anxiety, and (3) frequency of contact with the survivors' families of origin.

Characteristics of Interpersonal Behavior

The traditional emphasis on parents as the primary agents of socialization of children has overshadowed interest in the potential influence of siblings on each other. For the most part, family therapists and theorists tend to be more attuned to sibling relationships than are those from other schools. One such therapist, Salvador Minuchin, has described the sibling "subsystem" as a "social laboratory" where children experiment with peer relationships:

> Within this context, children support, isolate, scapegoat, and learn from each other. In the sibling world, children learn how to negotiate, cooperate and compete. They learn how to make friends and allies, how to save face while submitting, and how to achieve recognition of their skills.[6]

A theorist concerned with systems and their "boundaries," Minuchin stresses the need for a protective boundary around the sibling subsystem "so they can exercise their right to privacy, have their own areas of interest and be free to fumble as they explore."[7]

Bank and Kahn have also looked at qualitative aspects of the sibling relationship. They believe that influential sibling relationships occur only under certain circumstances. Specifically, "sibling bonds will become intense and exert a formative influence upon personality when, as children or adolescents, the siblings have had plentiful access and contact *and* have been deprived of reliable parental care."[8] In other words, Bank and Kahn believe that when relationships with alternative significant others are strong, the sibling bond will be weaker. This view fails to take into account that the sibling relationship has its own independent merits and that a child may have valuable relationships with siblings in addition to his or her relationships with adults. In an optimal—that is, friendly yet nonintrusive—relationship with caring but unpossessive adults, a child will naturally gravitate toward strong relationships with siblings and/or peers for what those additional relationships can offer.

The most useful information on the sibling relationship may come from analysis of animal behavior rather than from human subject research. In working with rhesus monkeys, Harlow[9] and Suomi and Harlow[10] have been able to observe and describe a "peer affectional system" from which they believe we can learn more about our comparable human system. Suomi and Harlow believe that although mother love is essential for the development of basic trust and security, "probably the most pervading and important of all the affectional systems in terms of long-range personal-social adjustments is the age-mate or peer affectional system."[11]

It is through peer play that the infant monkey learns to transfer the basic trust established in the mother-child love system to age-mates: "Social and cultural patterns are learned, control of aggression is accomplished, and the foundations are laid for later sex-appropriate behavior."[12] The early peer group for monkeys may be siblings or more often, probably, a mixture of relations and nonrelations of the same approximate age. Harlow stresses that through peer play, infant monkeys acquire the skills necessary for heterosexual relationships and successful sexual functioning. Monkeys who are deprived of adequate peer contact during their youth are fearful and aggressive when faced with heterosexual overtures. Suomi and Harlow's theory implies that a similar process may be at work in human peer/sibling relationships. Specifically, it suggests that peer/sibling contact is essential for the development of comfortable heterosexual relationships in humans.

Both Minuchin and Harlow perceive the sibling relationship as a unique and independent bond. While Minuchin stresses the role of the sibling subsystem in the broad process of socialization of the child, Harlow emphasizes the influence of peer/sibling relationships on heterosexual behavior. If these theorists are correct, then we might ask whether the loss of a sibling may not also have a profound influence on socialization and on heterosexual behavior. In other words, does sibling loss affect the development of these two facets of interpersonal behavior in survivors? One way of approaching the answer to this question is to examine interpersonal characteristics in those who have undergone a loss in childhood.

The California Psychological Inventory

The California Psychological Inventory (CPI) was developed by Harrison G. Gough in 1957 as a means of assessing "interpersonal behavior and dispositions relevant to social interaction."[13] This test was not constructed as a measure of abnormality (psychopathology) but rather for the assessment and clarification of personality characteristics that reveal themselves in everyday social living. It consists of 480 true/false items, which are contained in a test booklet (respondents mark their answers on special answer sheets). Completion of the test requires between 45 and 90 minutes, depending on the respondent's pace. The resultant "inventory" breaks down into eighteen scales, each measuring some theme (folk myth) or aspect of interpersonal behavior. The scales are:

Dominance (Do)

Capacity for status (Cs)

Sociality (Sy)

Social presence (Sp)

Self-acceptance (Sa)

Sense of well-being (Wb)

Responsibility (Re)

Socialization (So)

Self-control (Sc)

Flexibility (Fx)

Femininity (Fe)

Tolerance (To)

Good impression (Gi)

Communality (Cm)

Achievement via conformance (Ac)

Achievement via independence (Ai)

Intellectual efficiency (Ie)

Psychological-mindedness (Py)

The CPI has been widely tested for reliability and validity and has been utilized extensively as a research tool. While most often administered as a predictive measure, it has also been used as a means of examining personality differences among populations.[14]

The CPI was administered to the thirty four surviving siblings who participated in personal interviews and to a comparison group of thirty eight individuals who were graduate social work students and were comparable to the surviving siblings in age, sex, ethnicity, and socioeconomic status. Scores were also compared to norm scores for each measure. Finally, a comparison was made between those individuals who communicated about the loss at the time it occurred (the "expressive" group) and those who did not (the "nonexpressive" group). These comparisons were tested for statistical significance using the t-test, a measure of the significance of the variance between two sets of means.

Dominance and Self-Control in Surviving Siblings

The CPI yielded significant results on two characteristics of interpersonal behavior, *dominance* and *self-control*. Specifically, it was found that:

1. The group that had experienced sibling loss scored above the norm for dominance and significantly higher than the comparison group (significant at .05).

2. The group that communicated about their loss at the time (the expressive group) scored below the norm on self-control and significantly lower than the nonexpressive group (also significant at .05).

To understand these findings, it is necessary to examine what the concepts of dominance and self-control imply within the context of the CPI. The concept of dominance does not necessarily equate with the commonsense understanding of the word. Gough explains:

First, although the term "dominance" may suggest negative or "domineering" dominance, the scale is almost entirely free of such connotations. High scorers on Do are constructively dominant, and one of the cardinal features of their own introspections is an appeal to socially valid and worthwhile goals as a way of justifying their (occasionally) coercive behavior toward others. Dominance, in other words, is not an end in itself but a means by which one's group can be influenced toward more rational and more moral actions.[15]

In certain settings, a high scorer may follow rather than lead "and in so doing will dedicate himself to carrying out the wishes and mandates of the leader with the same indefatigable purposiveness that he displays on those occasions when he himself is in command."[16] In the preceding excerpt, the phrases "worthwhile goals" and "more moral actions" particularly stand out with respect to adults who have lost a sibling in childhood, because if surviving siblings can be said to have reported any "benefit" from their loss, it can best be expressed as that which brought them closer to values and goals that extend beyond their immediate gain. Respondents expressed this in a variety of ways, such as the following:

And yet, I think the loss gave me more compassion for, understanding of, and sensitivity toward others than I might have had if I had not gone through those years of agony brought by the loss. . . . I do think I have learned a great deal from his death and am now much stronger and more mature in many ways because of it . . . I now have a more heightened awareness of the reality of death and the need to make the best use of my life in the here and now.

I now live each day as if it may be someone's last. I won't part with anyone in anger; I want to leave them knowing that I care. I think that I have become a more caring person because of my experience. I am a better listener, and more considerate.

We (my family) have all reacted similarly in some ways: studying the illness, joining organizations, taking up charitable work in the field, working to solve the few parts of the problem that can be solved (such as providing decent physical care or earning extra money to pay for good medical help).

I also feel that having had and lost her has made me a more understanding person and a better wife and mother—I value my husband and children greatly because I know how fragile life is.

These excerpts seem to reflect the concept of dominance as a tendency toward socially valid and worthwhile goals and more rational, moral actions. For some, the loss of a sibling in childhood seemed to bring about a "heightened awareness" of new values and of what's "really" important in life, and motivated them toward actions in that direction. It is important to restate here that because the adult survivors in this study were not randomly selected from the population but rather were primarily self-selected, the findings are evidence only of this group's responses, and the representativeness of the data is unknown. Generalization of the findings must await corroboration through further research.

In terms of self-control, the individuals who did express feelings about the loss scored lower on this characteristic than did their nonexpressive counterparts. In fact, the expressive group scored significantly lower (23.2) than a sample reported by Gough of 7,150 females (32.0), and also lower than subgroups in that sample of high school disciplinary problems (23.9) and prison inmates (25.7).[17] This suggests that the nonexpressive group was not "overcontrolled" but in fact more representative of the general population than the expressive group. While these data demonstrate that communication about the loss may be linked to less self-control in the surviving sibling, they do not necessarily indicate a cause-and-effect relationship. It is possible that less self-control was a personality characteristic present in the surviving siblings at the time of the loss that may have accounted, in part, for their ability to talk about the loss.

Intimacy in Surviving Siblings

Degree of comfort in relationships with the opposite sex was examined in the interviews conducted with adult survivors of sibling loss. A questionnaire was used to measure various factors in relationships with peers and the family of origin (see Appendix C for complete questionnaire). Question #21 explored the degree of ease with which respondents experienced heterosexual relationships by asking, "Do you think that friendships with people of the same sex are easier than friendships with the opposite sex?"[18] Answering yes to this question was scored with a 1 and answering no was scored with a 2.

Table 7–1 reveals the findings for this question when comparing those

Table 7–1
"Do you think that friendships with people of the same sex are easier than friendships with the opposite sex?"

	N	Mean	Standard Deviation
"Expressive" group	8	1.9	.354
"Nonexpressive" group	26	1.4	.508

Significant at .02.

who communicated their feelings about the loss with those who did not. The table shows that adult survivors who were expressive about the loss were more likely to answer no to the question, while those who were not expressive were more likely to answer yes. While the difference in sample size necessitates extreme caution in interpretation, the findings do appear to suggest a relationship between expression of feelings of loss and ease in heterosexual relationships. One might argue that *if* a child is unable to express feelings concerning the loss of a sibling, *and* if this lack of expression interferes with mourning the loss, then *perhaps* the failure to mourn will have consequences for the child's ability in adulthood to invest in heterosexual relationships. The following example illustrates:

> Jane T. is a twenty-eight-year-old, attractive, white lawyer who sought counseling because of difficulties in her relationships with men. Her primary complaint was that she repeatedly became involved with inappropriate and/or unavailable men, while she consciously wished to marry and have a family. Over the course of (brief) treatment she realized that a serious relationship with an appropriate man generated a deep feeling of disloyalty toward her deceased brother, with whom she had been very close. As she mourned her brother more fully, she also began to terminate a relationship of two years with an already married man. A follow-up call one year later indicated that Jane was engaged to be married.

Death Anxiety in Survivors of Sibling Loss

In attempting to understand why some people fear death more than others do, intuition suggests that exposure to death is a factor. However, evidence available to us at the present time is inconclusive on this question. While there appears to be no relationship between the fear of death and the death of a close friend or relative within the preceding five years,[19] it is possible that exposure to death results in some increase in the fear of loss of consciousness.[20] Death anxiety in adult survivors of childhood sibling loss was measured through use of the Death Anxiety Questionnaire (DAQ) developed by Conte, Bakur-Weiner, and Plutchik.[21] The DAQ has been used to measure levels of death anxiety in college students, senior citizens, and nursing home residents[22] as well as in normal children and adolescents.[23] It is comprised of fifteen entries that describe possible concerns about death. A person responding to the questionnaire indicates whether he or she worries about each entry not at all, sometimes, or very much. The answers receive scores of 0, 1, or 2 and are compiled into scores ranging from 0, meaning that the respondent is not at all worried about any entry, to 30, signifying that he or she is very much worried about all fifteen entries. Groups of individuals taking the test

Table 7–2
Comparison of Scores for Death Anxiety
Questionnaire

Sample	Average Score
Junior high school students	7.99
Comparison group	8.15
Senior high school students	11.05
Adult survivors	11.38

have generally scored in the range of 7.36 to 9.58,[24] with a low average score of 7.99 reported for high school students and a high average score of 11.05 reported for senior high school students.[25] Table 7–2 compares these two scores with the average scores for the adult survivors of childhood sibling loss and the comparison group. The difference in scores for the latter two groups is significant at .01. The average score for the adult survivors of childhood sibling loss is the highest for all groups reported thus far, indicating that this group is more worried about death than the other groups that have been studied. The two primary questions on the DAQ that specifically triggered anxiety about death were #12, "Does the thought of leaving loved ones behind when you die disturb you?" which ranked number one, followed by #2, "Does it bother you that you may die before you have done everything you wanted to do?" These are the most commonly reported fears of death when this questionnaire had been used to measure death anxiety. Thus it appears that the surviving siblings do not report *different* concerns about death, but more anxiety about the most commonly expressed concerns.

Frequency of Contact with Family of Origin

Finally, the study examined frequency of contact between adult survivors of childhood sibling loss and their families of origin. Included in the questionnaire were a number of items dealing with current relationships between the surviving siblings and their brother(s), sister(s), and parents, in particular, the frequency of contact between the surviving siblings, their mother, father, and closest (or only) sibling. Respondents were asked to indicate daily, once or twice a week, once or twice a month, occasionally (that is, for holidays, funerals, and so forth), never, or deceased.[26] The answers of the surviving siblings were compared to those of the comparison group of adults who had not lost a sibling, and they were also broken down into the two groups of expressive and nonexpressive survivors. Scores were obtained by assigning a number between 1 and 6 to each answer, beginning with the most contact

Table 7–3
Average Frequency of Contact with Family of Origin

	Contact with Father[a]	Contact with Mother[b]	Contact with Sibling(s)[c]
"Expressive" survivors (N = 8)	Once or twice a month (2.7)	Once or twice a week (1.6)	Once or twice a month (2.4)
"Nonexpressive" survivors (N = 26)	Occasionally (4)	Once or twice a month (3)	Occasionally (4)

[a]Not significant.
[b]Significant at .001.
[c]Significant at .05.

(daily = 1) to the least contact (deceased = 6). Table 7–3 shows the findings for this question. While there was not a significant difference in the average contact of the expressive and non-expressive groups with their fathers, the nonexpressive group did report less contact. Regarding contact with mother and siblings, on the other hand, there were statistically significant differences between the two groups of adult survivors. Contact with mothers was more frequent—once or twice a week—among individuals in the expressive group than among those in the nonexpressive group, who had, on the average, monthly contact with their mothers. The expressive group also had more frequent contact with a sibling—once or twice a month—than did the nonexpressive group, which experienced only occasional contact. There was no difference in overall frequency of contact between the group of adult survivors and the comparison group.

There appears, then, to be a relationship between siblings' expression of feeling about the loss of a sister or brother at the time the loss occurs and frequency of contact between the adult survivors and their parents and siblings. Contact in the past also increases the likelihood of contact in the present. It is possible that we have uncovered a dimension of family behavior (that is, the expressive versus nonexpressive style) which affects mourning in children. Whether this is the case remains to be corroborated, but it does appear that bereaved families who value frequent contact beyond the child-rearing years would benefit from assistance in communicating together about the death of the child.

Summary

This chapter has presented findings in three areas related to adult survivors of childhood sibling loss: (1) characteristics of interpersonal behavior, (2) death anxiety, and (3) frequency of contact with family of origin. In brief, the data indicated that surviving siblings tended to rate high in the interpersonal characteristic of dominance; that the expressive group of surviving siblings tended to be low on self-control and more comfortable in heterosexual relationships; that the surviving sibling group had a higher level of death anxiety than other population groups that have been studied; and that expression of feelings about the loss at the time it occurs correlates with more frequent contact with parents and siblings in later years.

As we explore the long-range impact of childhood sibling loss, it becomes apparent that if we are to achieve the same level of understanding and knowledge that exists for other kinds of bereavement, we must first acknowledge to a far greater degree the importance of the sibling relationship and the potential impact of its disruption.

In the next and final chapter, we will examine ways in which children and their families can be helped to cope with the loss of a child.

Notes

1. For a critical review of research methodologies utilized in studies of childhood parental bereavement, see E. Markusen and R. Fulton, "Childhood Bereavement and Behavior Disorders: A Critical Review," *OMEGA: Journal of Death and Dying* 2 (1971): 107–17.

2. S. Rosenzweig and D. Bray, "Sibling Deaths in the Anamneses of Schizophrenic Patients," *Archives of Neurology and Psychiatry* 49 (1943): 71–92.

3. G. Pollock, "Bertha Pappenheim's Pathological Mourning," *Journal of American Psychoanalytical Association* 20 (1972): 476–93; idem, "On Siblings, Childhood Sibling Loss and Creativity," *Annual of Psychoanalysis,* vol. 6 (New York: International University Press, 1978).

4. I. Hilgard, "Depressive and Psychotic States as Anniversaries to Sibling Death in Childhood," *International Psychiatry Clinics* 6 (1969): 197–211.

5. See, for example, A. Beck, B. Sethi, and R. Tuthill, "Childhood Bereavement and Adult Depression," *Archives of General Psychiatry* 9 (1963): 295–302.

6. S. Minuchin, *Families and Family Therapy* (Cambridge: Harvard University Press, 1974), 59.

7. Ibid.

8. S. Bank and M. Kahn, *The Sibling Bond* (New York: Basic Books, 1982).

9. H. Harlow, *Learning to Love* (San Francisco, Albion Publishing, 1971).

10. S. Suomi and H. Harlow, "The Role and Reason of Peer Relationships in Rhesus Monkeys," in *Friendship and Peer Relations,* ed. L. Rosenblum (New York: John Wiley, 1975), 153–85.

11. Ibid., 49–50.

12. H. Harlow, *Learning to Love,* 101.

13. H. Gough, "An Interpreter's Syllabus for the California Psychological Inventory," in *Advances in Psychological Assessment,* vol. 1 (Palo Alto: Science and Behavior Books, 1968), 55–79.

14. See, for example, G.W. Durflinger, "Academic and Personality Differences

Between Women Students Who Do Complete the Elementary Teaching Credential Program and Those Who Do Not," *Educational and Psychological Measurement* 23 (1963): 383–90.

15. Gough, "An Interpreter's Syllabus," 59.

16. Ibid.

17. H. Gough, *Manual for the California Psychological Inventory* (Palo Alto: Consulting Psychologists Press, 1975), 32–33.

18. Adapted from a question constructed by Joel D. Block in *Friendship* (New York: Macmillan Publishing Co., 1980).

19. D. Lester and G. Kam, "Effect of a Friend Dying Upon Attitudes Toward Death," *Journal of Social Psychology* 83 (1971): 149–50.

20. J. Hoelter and J. Hoelter, "On Interrelationships Among Exposure to Death and Dying, Fear of Death and Anxiety," *OMEGA: Journal of Death and Dying*, 11, no. 3 (1980–81), 247.

21. H. Conte, M. Bakur-Weiner, and R. Plutchik, "Measuring Death Anxiety: Conceptual, Psycho-metric and Factor-analytic Aspects," *Journal of Personality and Social Psychology* 43, no. 4 (1982): 775–85.

22. H. Conte, M. Bakur-Weiner, R. Plutchik, and R. Bennett, "Development and Evaluation of a Death Anxiety Questionnaire," Proceedings of 83rd Annual Meeting of the American Psychology Association, Chicago, 1975.

23. G. Koocher, J. O'Malley, D. Foster, and I. Gogan, "Death Anxiety in Normal Children and Adolescents," *Psychiatria Clinica* 9 (1976): 220–29.

24. Conte, Bakur-Weiner, and Plutchik, "Measuring Death Anxiety: Conceptual, Psycho-metric and Factor-analytic Aspects," 775–85.

25. Koocher, O'Malley, Foster, and Gogan, "Death Anxiety in Normal Children and Adolescents," 220–29.

26. Adapted from a question constructed by B. Lackie in "Family Correlates of Career Achievements in Social Work," Ph.D. diss., Rutgers University, 1982.

8
Helping Children Cope with Sibling Loss

> To weep is to make less the depth of grief.
> — Shakespeare, *Henry IV, Part II*

hildren live in a world not of their own making and are subject to influences beyond their control. If as parents or professionals we are interested in improving our children's quality of life, we must concern ourselves with their relationship to death. Certainly, the relationship is complex and troubling, and we face it only with great reluctance. At heart, we prefer to deny that there is any connection between death and our children.

Nonetheless, experience does not allow us to maintain this denial for very long. The death of a child or of someone close to a child is an event which most children will observe firsthand at some point. There is much that can be done to help these children cope with the life crisis death poses. In this chapter, we will look at how we can assist bereaved children in general, and survivors of sibling loss in particular, in their efforts to live with loss.

Helping Children Cope with Bereavement

Before examining the specific needs of survivors of childhood sibling loss, we need to review what we know regarding *all* children who have suffered a major loss in their lives. For example, we know that a child fares better when faced with the loss of a significant person in his or her life if there has been previous, less traumatic experience with loss.[1] The death of a bug, bird, or pet can provide a child with the opportunity to appreciate the irreversibility of death and with a concrete knowledge of the natural order of things that may lessen the shock effect produced by the death of someone he or she loves.[2]

It is also to a child's advantage to be prepared whenever possible for the impending loss of someone significant.[3] If death is foreseen, children can be prepared for it to some degree by the gradual accumulation of information about the loved one's condition and the opportunity to ask questions and consider beforehand the possibility of death. As a result, some desensitization and anticipatory mourning may occur; obviously, this is not always possible.

In any event, it is clearly beneficial to a child to be able to express his or her ideas, fantasies, and fears about death and to be in an environment that conveys acceptance of his or her need to communicate about the loss.[4] An atmosphere that forbids a child to express the range of emotions associated with death encourages suppression and/or repression—mechanisms which prevent the occurrence of a healthy process of mourning.[5]

Additionally, children need to be told what is happening or has happened, regarding a death, in language that is clear and age-appropriate.[6] Information which is provided must be consonant with the child's level of development and understanding of death. Metaphors (for example, equating death with shedding a cocoon) are often confusing to the concrete cognitive abilities of the child; likewise, religious conceptualizations ("your sister is with the Lord") may confuse the child; and references which equate death with sleep can easily cause the child to be anxious about sleeping.

An avenue for helping individual children cope with grief and loss is the bibliotherapy approach described by Bernstein.[7] Books dealing with various facets of loss can be made available to the child as an adjunct to other forms of assistance.

Participation in the Funeral

As stated earlier, there is general concurrence that children from the age of four on should be allowed to decide for themselves whether they will attend the funeral of a deceased family member.[8] Wessel provides the following guidelines for including children in funeral proceedings:

1. The child should be told in advance the details of what will transpire.
2. The child should be told that people will cry.
3. The child should be with a close friend or relative during the whole event so that he or she is not alone or isolated.
4. The child's wishes to attend all, part, or none of the ceremony should be honored.[9]

By attending the funeral, the child may receive two major benefits: he or she is afforded an opportunity to observe firsthand what death entails, while observation of "the expression of emotion that usually occurs at the funeral makes it easier for the child to express his own feelings."[10] On the other hand, attending a funeral may be overwhelming for the child.

When a Brother or Sister Dies

In addition to the general guidelines already presented for helping bereaved children, there are unique characteristics of sibling loss that suggest further ways of assisting this population. A summary of what we have learned from these characteristics follows.

It is important, first and foremost, that children who lose a sibling experience *acknowledgment of their loss,* preferably from their parents and immediate family members but also from extended family, neighbors, teachers, religious representatives, and others who come in contact with them. Failure to acknowledge the *child's* loss sets in motion the beginning of a response that inhibits (and prohibits) mourning in the child. Those who interact with a bereaved child may also be unaware of the differences between the ways adults and children express grief. For the observer, the adult's capacity for expression of feelings often overshadows the child's less obvious grief reaction, which leads to the erroneous conclusion that the child is not in great pain. In fact, the child may be experiencing a wide range of feelings connected to the loss, including sadness, grief, guilt, and an overburdening sense of responsibility to make up to the parents for their loss. These inner reactions will not be outwardly expressed, however, if those people who are around the child convey an attitude of unconcern.

Second, we need to look more closely at the reactions of the parents to the loss and the effects of these reactions on surviving siblings, as well as at the response of the whole family as a system to the loss of a member. We need to be aware of differences in the ways grieving parents respond to loss and of the potential for surviving siblings to feel abandoned by them. The death of a child may result in a fixation in the progression of the family life cycle and the inability of the family to assist surviving siblings with their developmental needs. Despite such a tragic event as the death of a child, the development of surviving siblings does not stop. They continue to need parents who can provide flexible and sensitive care and guidance. If parents become unable to provide these things, serious difficulties may develop in the family.

Third, greater awareness is necessary of the potential for conflict between the needs of bereaved parents and the needs of bereaved siblings—particularly in the tie-breaking/tie-maintaining aspect of mourning. In general, it is probably possible for both parents and siblings to engage in the kinds of activities that will help them accept and cope with their loss, as long as it is understood that these activities will be different.

Based on the findings presented in this book and in the related literature, the following recommendations can be made:

1. Family members should be encouraged and helped to communicate with each other about the loss—including the surviving siblings.

2. The bereaved community should also be encouraged and helped to communicate with the bereaved child about the loss. This implies a public effort to educate all who come into regular contact with children on the importance of their behavior with regard to bereaved children.

3. Individual family members should be encouraged to grieve in their own ways; families need to know that their members will grieve differently but that all ways are legitimate and useful. This means that surviving siblings would be allowed to immerse themselves in school-related activities and to retain mementos of the deceased; that they would be included, if they so desire, in services and other gatherings where they would observe the grief, as well as the support, of the community; and that they would be able to express religious faith when it is present. Helping professionals should also be aware of and on the lookout for feelings in surviving siblings that indicate a need to make up to the parents for the loss they have experienced. Children who feel this way need to be told that no one can make up for the loss of another individual and that they can only continue to be themselves.

4. With regard to further research, the study points to a need to be more fully aware of the tendency of children to adapt their responses to loss to the expectations of those around them. Repression, suppression, denial of feelings or failure to express feelings may be the result, at least partially, of the child's sensitivity to cues in the environment that prohibits him or her from awareness or expression of feelings, or both. Failure to acknowledge this dynamic may cause us to develop less than adequate explanations of childhood bereavement.

Implications for Adult Survivors

For adults who have experienced the loss of a sibling in childhood, we have seen that three issues may be of significance: intimacy in surviving siblings, death anxiety, and frequency of contact with the family of origin. It should be noted, though, that the death of a sibling in childhood is not something that adult survivors generally discuss. In fact, it is highly likely that a number of individuals known to the reader have experienced such a loss without ever having shared that information. The same may be true for surviving siblings who seek mental health services or other assistance from the helping professions. Adult survivors often *appear* to have adapted the prevailing attitude that their loss was not highly significant, but on closer examination, it will be discovered that this is not reflective of their true feelings about the loss.

At any rate, the present study suggests that long-term consequences of childhood sibling loss may appear in the form of less ease in heterosexual relationships, possibly greater death anxiety, and less frequent contact between the adult survivor and his or her family of origin, especially with the mother. On the positive side, adult survivors may rate higher than average on the trait of dominance as it is defined in chapter 7. While the present study has not proven a relationship between these factors and childhood sibling loss, their potentiality as significant issues in the lives of adult survivors should be explored, particularly if it becomes apparent that there was an inadequate opportunity to mourn the loss in childhood.

Siblings of Terminally Ill Children

The literature on siblings of children with terminal or life-threatening illness clearly documents the need for greater concern and services for this population.

Once again it should be stated that the most important factor in helping the siblings of terminally ill children is acknowledgment of the significance of this circumstance in their lives. In addition, these siblings benefit from knowledge of their siblings' illness and its treatment, and from the opportunity to express their fears and concerns. Kramer and Moore describe a program developed at the Pediatric Hematology-Oncology Department at the University of California, San Francisco, to educate siblings of cancer patients.[11] The program described earlier at Cooper Hospital/University Medical Center focused primarily on the need for expression of concerns and feelings. Evans, Combrinck-Graham, and Ross remind us in their program of the need to focus at specific critical times on the siblings of cancer patients.[12] These programs and others like them that are being developed in hospitals and clinics across the country are evidence of the helping profession's response to a growing awareness of the need to direct services to siblings. For the family, which is often already overburdened with meeting the needs of the ill child, participation in services for the healthy siblings is not always easy. But the effort to participate is rewarded with the sibling's greater capacity to understand and cope with the painful reality of childhood sibling loss.

Helping the Bereaved Family

There is wide variation among families in their ability to cope with the loss of a member and in their styles of coping. Specifically, three kinds of families have been identified in this regard: (1) families in which there is a cohesive cultural subgroup, where family and friends aid each other and meet the needs of the bereaved family members, (2) isolated families, atomized and nuclear, with limited social contacts, and (3) atomized nuclear families who are used to depending on professionals and experts to guide and support them. The need for and openness to involvement with outside agencies is greatest for this last group. The involvement is needed but generally unwanted in the second group, and unnecessary and ornamental in the first group.[13] It is important also to note that while the role of mental health clinics in helping people cope with loss is growing, on account of our society's failure to support bereavement needs, most of this assistance is offered in the form of individual treatment, which often fails to address issues of the bereaved family as a social unit.[14] Certainly, further development of our understanding of family responses to bereavement is needed. A family's failure to mourn the death of a member may leave a "ghost" in the family, which prevents the surviving members from beginning "a new life."[15] Family intervention at the time of the loss may be most useful in assisting the family with the coping and adaptational tasks it faces. For surviving siblings, it may also open the door to family acknowledgment of their grief and need to mourn.

Death as a Social Phenomenon

The overriding issue that faces us all in our determination to cope with loss and to help others cope with loss is the place accorded to death in our lives today and in the world we live in. Throughout history, human beings have struggled with the fear of unknown death, with the reality of their own mortality, with the problem of living with the knowledge of personal death. Quotations from de la Rochefoucauld—"one cannot look directly at either the sun or death"—and Seneca—"no man enjoys the true taste of life but he who is willing and ready to quit it"—are offered by Dumont and Foss as representative of our alternating attitudes of denial and acceptance of death.[16] In our current belief system, which emphasizes mastery over nature, death is often viewed as "an accident, a mistake, a momentary failure for mankind as if it were fully believed that given time to plan, much hard work, and the application of scientific principle, man will ultimately prevail."[17] Perhaps a further indication of current attitudes toward death is our willingness to view bereavement as a sickness, to relinquish personal responsibility for caring for our bereaved in favor of "professional intervention." Useful and necessary as that intervention may be, it is also a commentary on the meaning and quality of our present society and the absence of adequate social networks (neighborhoods, cultural subgroups, extended family) to help each of us cope with an intrinsic aspect of our existence.

Anthropologists are fond of pointing out ways in which more primitive societies cope with issues of living that modern society fails to adequately address, and death is certainly a case in point. Funeral rituals in some older, traditional societies are directed toward aiding mourners in accepting death, feeling less isolated, and reentering society.[18] Such traditions still exist for some segments of our society, but for many others they are sorely lacking. Turning over the management of grief and mourning to mental health professionals has also proved inadequate. Therapists tend to avert discussion of death and to not acknowledge allusions to death anxiety. A product of our society, mental health practitioners are often "ill prepared culturally, professionally, theoretically, and attitudinally to deal with death material."[19] Until these attitudes change at the societal level, we will not see real change in how individuals and families cope with loss. As long as we view death as an accident, and overt expression of grief and mourning as an ominous occurrence, we will be alienated and disengaged from the meaning of life.

Children's reactions to the loss of a brother or sister is only one arena in which this conflict is played out. Death is always difficult. But, in the words of Rainer Maria Rilke, "We must always hold to the difficult."

> But only someone who is ready for everything, who excludes nothing, not even the most enigmatical, will live the relation to another as something alive and will himself draw exhaustively from his own existence. . . . We are set down in life as in the element to which we best correspond . . . scarcely to be distinguished from all that surrounds us.[20]

Notes

1. S. Salladay and M. Royal, "Children and Death: Guidelines for Grief Work," *Child Psychiatry and Human Development* 11, no. 4 (1981): 203–12.

2. R. Gardner, "Children's Reactions to Parental Death," in *The Child and Death*, ed. J. Schowalter et al., (New York: Columbia University Press, 1983).

3. M. Mahler, "Helping Children to Accept Death," *Child Study* (Fall 1950): 98–120.

4. Ibid.; Salladay and Royal, "Children and Death: Guidelines for Grief Work," 203–12.

5. Gardner, "Children's Reactions to Parental Death," 114–15.

6. Mahler, "Helping Children to Accept Death," 98–120; Salladay and Royal, "Children and Death: Guidelines for Grief Work," 203–12.

7. J. Bernstein, *Books to Help Children Cope with Separation and Loss* (New York: R.R. Bowher, 1977).

8. M. Wessel, "Children, When Parents Die," in *The Child and Death*, ed. J. Schowalter et al., (New York: Columbia University Press, 1983).

9. Ibid.

10. Gardner, "Children's Reactions to Parental Death," 109.

11. R. Kramer and I. Moore, "Childhood Cancer: Meeting the Special Needs of Healthy Siblings," *Cancer Nursing* (June 1983): 213–17.

12. A. Evans, R. Combrinck-Graham, and J. Ross, "Meeting the Problems of Siblings of a Child with Cancer," Paper presented at the American Cancer Society 2nd Annual Conference on Human Values and Cancer, Chicago, September 1977.

13. R. Vollman, A. Ganzert, L. Picher, and W. Williams, "The Reactions of Family Systems to Sudden and Unexpected Death," *OMEGA: Journal of Death and Dying* 2 (1971): 101–6.

14. Ibid.

15. E. Gelcer, "Mourning Is a Family Affair," *Family Process* 22 (1983): 501–76.

16. R. Dumont and D. Foss, *The American View of Death* (Cambridge: Schenkman Publishing Co., 1972), 33.

17. E. Bermann, "Death Terror: Observations of Interaction Patterns in an American Family," *OMEGA: Journal of Death and Dying* 4, no. 4 (1973): 283.

18. H. Goldberg, "Funeral and Bereavement Rituals of Kota Indians and Orthodox Jews," *OMEGA: Journal of Death and Dying* 12, no. 2 (1981–82): 117–28.

19. Bermann, "Death Terror: Observations of Interaction Patterns in an American Family," 281.

20. R.M. Rilke, *Letters to a Young Poet,* translated by M.D. Herter Norton, 69. Copyright 1934 by W.W. Norton & Company, Inc. Copyright renewed 1962 by M.D. Herter Norton. Revised edition copyright 1954 by W.W. Norton & Company, Inc., reprinted with permission.

Epilogue

While in the process of writing this book, my good friend and colleague Hace Tishler passed away. His death was sudden, and certainly untimely. A few weeks later, some of his friends gathered at one couple's home to share memories and thoughts of this unusual person who is no longer with us. One of us remarked that Hace would have been upset that we met this way, without him—he hated to miss a party!

I am grateful to those friends who were present that morning to "speak the name" of Hace. I miss Hace and think of him often—fondly, and with love.

Appendix A:
Survey Questionnaire

Socioeconomic Data

1. Age _____

2. Sex _____

3. Religion _____

4. Ethnicity _____

5. Occupation _____

6. Place of residence (city, state) _____

7. Marital status—check one:

   Married or remarried _____
   Separated _____
   Widowed _____
   Divorced _____

8. Number of children _____

Circumstances of Sibling Death

9. What was *your* age at the time of your sibling's death? _____

10. How old was your sibling? _____

11. Did you lose a brother or a sister? _____

12. How did your sibling die?

13. How did you find out about the death?

14. Did you have any other siblings at the time of the death? If so, how many?

    brother(s) _____   sister(s) _____

15. Did you attend services for your sibling? _____

Reactions to Sibling Loss

16. Please describe, to whatever extent you feel comfortable, how you felt as a *child* when your sibling died.

17. Do you feel that the loss of your sibling changed your relationship with other family members, especially your parents and other siblings? If so, how?

18. Do you feel that the loss of your sibling influenced your choice of occupation or the way you raise your own children (if applicable)? If so, how?

19. Do you feel that the loss of your sibling affected your performance in school at any time? If so, how?

20. Do you feel that the loss of your sibling influenced the way you get along with people outside your family, for instance, your friends, coworkers, spouse, and so forth? If so, how?

21. Did you ever seek professional help in relation to your sibling's death (counseling, psychotherapy, etc.)?

22. What effect, if any, do you feel that your sibling's death had on the rest of your family—your parents and other siblings (if any)?

23. How do you feel about the loss today?

Thank you.

Appendix B:
Socioeconomic Characteristics of
Survey Population

Characteristics	Survey Population (N = 159)	Interview Sample (N = 34)
Age		
Range	15–74	17–64
Mean	36	37
Sex		
Male	16%	9%
Female	84%	91%
Race		
White	93%	100%
Other	7%	—
Religion		
Protestant	41%	38%
Catholic	32%	32%
Jewish	19%	21%
Unaffiliated	7%	9%
Marital status		
Married or remarried	60%	59%
Single (never married)	29%	29%
Separated, widowed, or divorced	11%	12%
Children		
None	44%	47%
1	13%	9%
2	24%	21%
3	11%	21%
4+	9%	3%
Occupation		
Professional/white collar	43%	29%
Student/houseperson	23%	36%

Characteristics	Survey Population (N = 159)	Interview Sample (N = 34)
Secretarial/clerical/sales	18%	21%
Blue collar	6%	5%
Proprietor, manager	6%	9%
Unemployed/retired	4%	—
Residence		
Massachusetts	31%	—
New Jersey	23%	32%
Pennsylvania	21%	65%
Other (California, South Carolina, New Hampshire, Florida, etc.)	25%	3%

Appendix C:
Interview Questionnaire

Part I: Background Data

This section is concerned with you and your family background. Please make a check in the space to the left of your answer.

1. Sex: _____

2. Age:

   _____ 18–21
   _____ 22–25
   _____ 26–29
   _____ 30–34
   _____ 35–39
   _____ 40–44
   _____ 45–49
   _____ 50–54
   _____ 55–59
   _____ 60–64
   _____ 65 and above

3. Religion

   _____ Protestant
   _____ Catholic
   _____ Jewish
   _____ Moslem
   _____ Buddhist
   _____ Other
   _____ None

4. Ethnicity:

    _____ Caucasian
    _____ Afro-American
    _____ Hispanic
    _____ American-Indian
    _____ Asian-American
    _____ Other. Please specify. _____

5. By whom were you raised?

    _____ Natural parents
    _____ Natural mother only
    _____ Natural father only
    _____ Adoptive parents
    _____ Other. Please specify. _____

6. Level of education:

    _____ Some high school
    _____ Graduated high school
    _____ Graduated college
    _____ Some graduate school
    _____ Completed graduate school

7. Marital status:

    _____ Single
    _____ Married
    _____ Divorced, separated
    _____ Widowed
    _____ Remarried
    _____ Living with someone in a romantic relationship

8. How many children do you have?

    _____ 0
    _____ 1
    _____ 2
    _____ 3
    _____ 4
    _____ 5
    _____ 6+

9. What is your occupation?

    _____ Houseperson

_____ Student
_____ Unskilled worker
_____ Skilled or semiskilled worker
_____ Farmer or farm manager
_____ Clerical, secretarial, or sales
_____ Proprieter, manager, or official
_____ Professional

10. Which characterizes the marital status of your parents or other caretaker for most of the time *while you were growing up*?

_____ Married
_____ Divorced, separated
_____ Unmarried
_____ Widowed

11. Which characterizes the financial condition of your family for most of the time *while you were growing up*?

_____ Money was often a serious problem.
_____ Money was sometimes a serious problem.
_____ We weren't rich, but we had enough money for the necessities.
_____ We had enough money for the necessities of life and even for some luxuries.
_____ We had more than enough money at all times.

12. Read the paragraphs below, then check the one paragraph the *most closely* describes how your family got along together *while you were growing up*.

_____ There was a lot of freedom in my family and I pretty much could do my own thing. No one got upset if my grades were bad or I stayed out late. Some of my friends' parents were a lot stricter. If I became sick, I was still expected to go to school. I could easily lie to my parents.

_____ My parents had definite rules and the kids had to follow them. We could argue, but they usually won. As children, we were expected to take care of our rooms, our homework, etc. All the children had chores to do.

_____ We were a very close family—a lot of talking and sharing—we never closed our bedroom doors. If something bad happened to one of us, everyone became upset. My parents had a hard time enforcing rules, though. Often, we would have loud screaming matches. It was a very emotional household. Still, we'll always be very close.

Part II

This section concerns your relationship with your brothers and sisters (siblings). If you have never had any siblings, go to question 21.

13. On the chart below, mark an *X* on the *line* that indicates when *you* were born (ignore the parentheses ( ) for now).[a]

_____( ) _____( ) _____( ) _____( ) _____( ) _____( )
1st born   2nd born   3rd born   4th born   5th born   6th born

14. Now, on the same chart, write an *S* (for *sister*) or *B* (for *brother*) on the appropriate lines for each of your siblings. For example, if you are the second of three children, with an older and younger brother, your chart would look like this (include any siblings who are deceased).

___B__( ) ___X__( ) ___B__( ) _____( ) _____( ) _____( )
1st born   2nd born   3rd born   4th born   5th born   6th born

Use only the number of spaces you need. If you have more siblings than there are spaces for, please add the necessary spaces.

15. The last entry on the chart concerns the number of months or years separating each of your brothers and sisters. In the parentheses ( ) on the chart, fill in the number of months or years between each sibling. For instance, using the example from the last question, if the second-born child came eleven months after the first-born and the third child came two years after the second child, the chart would now look like this:

___B__(11 ms.) ___X__(2 yrs.) ___B__( ) _____( ) _____( ) _____( )
1st born   2nd born   3rd born   4th born   5th born   6th born

If you or any of your siblings are twins, indicate this by putting a *T* in the parentheses between the twins. The chart is now complete.

16. a. How many of your siblings did you feel close to *while you were growing up?* _____

  b. How many of your siblings do you feel close to *today?* _____

_____

[a]Adapted from a question by Bruce Lackie in "Family Correlates of Career Achievement in Social Work," Ph.D. diss., Rutgers University, 1982.

17. Which sibling was your favorite *while you were growing up*? (Check one.)

_____ first-born child
_____ second-born child
_____ third-born child
_____ fourth-born child
_____ fifth-born child
_____ sixth-born child

18. The following sentences describe some of the ways children feel about their brothers and sisters. Thinking back to *when you were growing up,* check those sentences that best describe how you and your *favorite* sibling got along.

_____ We told "little white lies" for one another.
_____ We competed for praise, recognition, attention.
_____ We were good friends.
_____ We spent a lot of time together.
_____ We taught each other many things.
_____ We protected and took care of each other.
_____ When we did something wrong, we would try to blame the other.
_____ I wasn't close to any of my siblings.

19. Now, using the same sentences (but in the present tense), along with some new ones, indicate how you feel about the same sibling today.

_____ We tell "little white lies" for one another.
_____ We compete for praise, recognition, attention.
_____ We are good friends.
_____ We spend a lot of time together.
_____ We teach each other many things.
_____ We protect and take care of each other.
_____ When we do something wrong, we try to blame the other.
_____ I am not close to that sibling anymore.
_____ I wasn't close to any of my siblings when I was growing up.
_____ That sibling is now deceased.

20. How often did you play with a sibling of the opposite sex?

_____ Never
_____ Rarely
_____ Sometimes
_____ Often

21. Do you think that friendships with people of the same sex are easier than friendships with the opposite sex?[b]

_____ Yes

_____ No

22. How often do you communicate with your family?

	Mother	Father	Closest or Only Sibling
Daily	_____	_____	_____
Once or twice a week	_____	_____	_____
Once or twice a month	_____	_____	_____
Occasionally (i.e., holidays, funerals, etc.)	_____	_____	_____
Never	_____	_____	_____
Deceased	_____	_____	_____

---

[b]Adapted from a question by Joel D. Block in *Friendship,* New York: Macmillan Publishing Co., 1980.

Appendix D:
Circumstances of Loss

Characteristics	Survey Population (N = 159)	Interview Sample (N = 34)
Age at time of loss		
−5	13%[a]	12%
6–12	42%	50%
13–16	27%	20%
17–19	18%	18%
Age of sibling who died		
−5	20%	18%
6–12	27%	26%
13–16	17%	24%
17–19	14%	12%
20–24	19%	12%
25+	3%	9%
Relationship of sibling to respondent		
Older vs. younger		
older sibling	60%[b]	62%
younger sibling	38%	38%
twin	2%	—
Brother vs. sister		
brother	64%[b]	59%
sister	36%	41%
Same vs. opposite sex		
opposite sex	57%[b]	62%
same sex	43%	38%
Cause of death		
Motor vehicle and other accidents (i.e., diving, swimming, fire)	34%	21%
Pneumonia, appendicitis, infections and related illnesses	25%	26%
Cancer	15%	20%
Birth defects and genetic disorders	9%	15%

Characteristics	Survey Population (N = 159)	Interview Sample (N = 34)
Suicide	7%	3%
War	4%	9%
Drug reactions or interactions	2%	—
Unknown causes	2%	3%
Sudden infant death syndrome	1%	3%
Died at birth	1%	—

Note: Percentage may not add up to 100, owing to rounding.

ᵃWhere respondent lost two siblings at different times, only data from first loss are included.

ᵇTwo respondents lost two siblings at same time—data included on both siblings.

Appendix E:
Projective Test

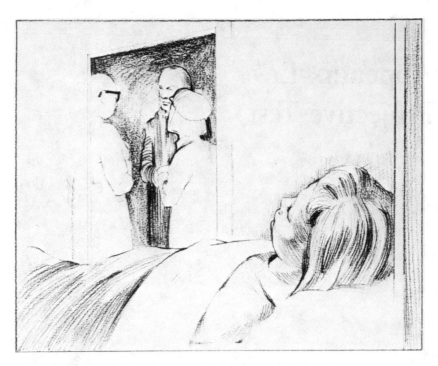

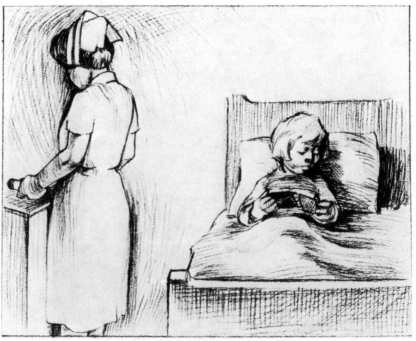

Appendix F:
Death Anxiety Questionnaire

Attitudes towards Death and Dying

Name or Code Number _____ Date _____

Sex _____

Age _____

Listed below are a number of questions concerning thoughts that people sometimes have about death and dying. Please indicate how much you worry about the things described by each of the questions.

	Not at All	*Sometimes*	*Very Much*
1. Do you worry about dying?	_____	_____	_____
2. Does it bother you that you may die before you have done everything you wanted to?	_____	_____	_____
3. Do you worry that you may be very ill for a long time before you die?	_____	_____	_____
4. Does it upset you to think that others may see you suffering when you die?	_____	_____	_____
5. Do you worry that dying may be very painful?	_____	_____	_____
6. Do you worry that the persons most close to you won't be with you when you are dying?	_____	_____	_____
7. Do you worry that you may be alone when you are dying?	_____	_____	_____
8. Does the thought bother you that you might lose control of your mind before death?	_____	_____	_____

	Not at All	Sometimes	Very Much
9. Do you worry that expenses connected with your dying will be a burden for other people?	————	————	————
10. Does it worry you that your instructions or will about your belongings may not be carried out after you die?	————	————	————
11. Are you afraid that you may be buried before you are really dead?	————	————	————
12. Does the thought of leaving loved ones behind when you die disturb you?	————	————	————
13. Do you worry that those you care about may not remember you after your death?	————	————	————
14. Does the thought worry you that with death you may be gone forever?	————	————	————
15. Are you worried about not knowing what to expect after death?	————	————	————

Bibliography

Adler, C. "The Meaning of Death to Children." *Arizona Medicine* 26, no. 3 (1969): 266–76.

Alexander, I., and A. Adlerstein. "Affective responses to the concept of death in a population of children and early adolescents." *Journal of Genetic Psychology* 93 (1958): 167–77.

Anthony, E., and Koupernick, C., eds. *The Child in His Family*. Yearbook of the International Association for Child Psychiatry and Allied Professions, vol. 2. New York: John Wiley, 1973.

Anthony, S. *The Discovery of Death in Childhood and After*. New York: Basic Books, 1972.

Arthur, B., and Kemme, M. "Bereavement in childhood." *Journal of Child Psychology and Psychiatry* 5 (1964): 37–49.

Atkinson, T. "Race as a factor in teachers' responses to children's grief." *OMEGA: Journal of Death and Dying* 13, no. 3 (1982–83): 243–50.

Baer, R. "The Sick Child Knows." In *Should the Patient Know the Truth?* edited by S. Standard and H. Nathan. New York: Springer, 1955.

Bakwin, H. "Suicide in children and adolescents." *Journal of Pediatrics* 50, no. 6 (1957): 749–69.

Banks, S., and Kahn, M. *The Sibling Bond*. New York: Basic Books, 1982.

Balk, D. "Adolescents' grief reactions and self-concept perceptions following sibling death: A study of 33 teenagers." *Journal of Youth and Adolescence* 12, no. 2 (1983): 137–60.

———. "Effects of sibling death on teenagers." *Journal of School Health* 53, no. 1 (1983): 14–18.

Barnes, M. "Reactions to the death of a mother." *Psychoanalytic Study of the Child* 19 (1964): 334–57.

Beck, A.; Sethi, B.; and Tuthill, R. "Childhood bereavement and adult depression." *Archives of General Psychiatry* 9 (1963): 295–302.

Becker, D., and Margolin, F. "How surviving parents handled their young children's adaptation to the crisis of loss." *American Journal of Orthopsychiatry* 37 (1967): 753–57.

Becker, E. *The Denial of Death*. New York: Free Press, 1973.

Bender, L. *A Dynamic Psychopathology of Childhood*. Springfield, Ill.: Charles C. Thomas, 1954.

Berezin, N. *After a Loss in Pregnancy—Help for Families Affected by a Miscarriage, a Stillbirth or the Loss of a Newborn*. New York: Simon & Schuster, 1982.

Binger, C. "Childhood leukemia—Emotional impact on siblings." In *The Child in His Family: The Impact of Death and Disease*, vol. 2, edited by E.J. Anthony and C. Koupernik. New York: John Wiley, 1973.

Binger, C.; Ablin, A.; Feuerstein, R.; Kushner, J.; Zager, S.; and Mikkelsen, C. "Childhood leukemia: Emotional impact on patient and family." *New England Journal of Medicine* 280 (1969): 414–18.

Blinder, B. "Sibling death in childhood." *Child Psychiatry and Human Development* 2 (1972): 169–75.

Bluebond-Langner, M. "Awareness and communication in terminally ill children: Pattern, process and pretense." Ph.D. diss., University of Illinois, 1975.

———. "Meanings of Death to Children." In *New Meanings of Death*, edited by H. Feifel. New York: McGraw-Hill, 1977.

———. *The Private World of Dying Children*. Princeton, N.J.: Princeton University Press, 1978.

Bowen, M. "Family Reaction to Death." In *Family Therapy: Theory and Practice*, edited by P. Guerin. New York: Gardner Press, 1976.

Bowlby, J. "Grief and mourning in infancy and early childhood." *Psychoanalytic Study of the Child* 15 (1960): 9–52.

———. "Childhood mourning and its implications for psychiatry." *American Journal of Psychiatry* 118 (1961): 481–98.

Bowlby, J., and Parkes, C. "Separation and loss within the family." In *The Child in His Family: The Impact of Death and Disease*, vol. 2, edited by E. Anthony and C. Koupernik. New York: John Wiley, 1973.

Brice, C. "Mourning through the life cycle." *American Journal of Psychoanalysis* 42, no. 2 (1982): 315–25.

Burton, L., ed. *Care of Child Facing Death*. London and Boston: Routledge & Kegan Paul, 1974.

Cain, A., and Cain, B. "On replacing a child." *Journal of the American Academy of Child Psychiatry* 3 (1964): 443–56.

Cain, A.; Fast, I.; and Erickson, M. "Children's disturbed reaction to the death of a sibling." *American Journal of Orthopsychiatry* 34 (1964): 741–52.

Cairns, N.U.; Clark, G.M.; Smith, S.D.; and Lansky, S.B. "Adaptation of siblings to childhood malignancies." *Journal of Pediatrics* 95 (1979): 484–87.

Cardarelle, J. "A group for children with deceased parents." *Social Work* 20, no. 4 (1975): 328–29.

Cho, S.A.; Freeman, E.M.; and Patterson, S.L. "Adolescents' experience with death: Practice implications." *Social Casework* 63, no. 2 (1982): 88–94.

Conte, H.; Bakur-Weiner, M.; Plutchik, R.; and Bennett, R. "Development and evaluation of a death anxiety questionnaire." Proceedings of the 83rd Annual Meeting of the American Psychological Association, Chicago, 1975.

Conte, H.; Bakur-Weiner, M.; and Plutchik, R. "Measuring death anxiety: Conceptual, psychometric and factor-analytic aspects." *Journal of Personality and Social Psychology* 43, no. 4 (1982): 775–85.

Cook, S. *Children and Dying: An Exploration and Selected Bibliographies*. New York: Health Sciences Publishing Corp., 1974.

Crase, D., and Crase, E. "Helping children understand death." *Young Children* 32, no. 1 (1976): 21–25.

Davids, A. "Personality and attitudes of child care workers, psychotherapist, and parents of children in residential treatment." *Child Psychiatry and Human Development* 1 (1970): 41–49.

Davis, J.A. "The attitude of parents to the approaching death of their child." *Developmental Medicine and Child Neurology* 6 (1964): 286–88.

Davoli, G. "The child's request to die at home." *Pediatrics* 38 (1966): 925.

Deutsch, H. "The absence of grief." *The Psychoanalytic Quarterly* 6 (1937): 12–22.

Diskin, M., and Guggenheim, H. "The child and death as seen in different cultures." In *Explaining Death to Children,* edited by E.A. Grollman. Boston: Beacon Press, 1967.

Dumont, R., and Foss, D. *The American View of Death.* Cambridge, Mass.: Schenkman Publishing Co., 1972.

Easson, E. *The Dying Child: The Management of the Child or Adolescent Who Is Dying.* Springfield, Ill.: Charles C. Thomas, 1970.

Elizur, E., and Kauffman, M. "Factors influencing the severity of childhood bereavement reactions." *American Journal of Orthopsychiatry* 53, no. 4 (1983): 668–76.

Evans, A. "If a child must die." *New England Journal of Medicine* 278, no. 3 (1968): 138–42.

Evans, A.; Combrinch-Graham, L.; and Ross, J. "Meeting the problems of siblings of a child with cancer." Paper presented at the American Cancer Society Second Annual Conference on Values and Cancer, Chicago, September 1977.

Freud, A. "Discussion of Dr. John Bowlby's paper." *Psychoanalytic Study of the Child* 25 (1960): 53–62.

Freud, S. *Totem and Taboo.* New York: Standard Edition, 1952.

———. "Mourning and melancholia." In *General Psychological Theory.* New York: Collier Books, 1963.

Freulund, D. "Children and death from the school setting viewpoint." *Journal of School Health* 47, no. 9 (1977): 533–37.

Fulton, R. *Death and Identity.* New York: John Wiley & Sons, 1965.

Furman, E. *A Child's Parent Dies.* New Haven: Yale University Press, 1974.

———. "Studies in childhood bereavement." *Canadian Journal of Psychiatry* 28, no. 4 (1983): 241–47.

Furman, R. "Death and the young child." *Psychoanalytic Study of the Child* 19 (1964): 321–33.

———. "The child's reaction to death in the family." In *Loss and Grief: Psychological Management in Medical Practice,* edited by B. Schoenberg et al. New York: Columbia University Press, 1970.

Gardner, R. "Children's reactions to parental death." In *The Child and Death,* edited by J. Schowalter et al. New York: Columbia University Press, 1983.

Gartley, W., and Bernasconi, M. "The concept of death in children." *Journal of Genetic Psychology* 110 (1967): 71–85.

Gauthier, Y. "The mourning reaction of a ten-and-a-half-year-old boy." *Psychoanalytic Study of the Child* 20 (1965): 481–94.

———. "The mourning reaction of a ten-year-old boy." *Canadian Psychiatric Asso-*

ciation Journal 11 (Supplement, 1966): 307–8.

Gay, M., and Tonge, W. "The late effects of loss of parents in childhood." *British Journal of Psychiatry* 113 (1967): 753–59.

Geertinger, P. *Sudden Death in Infancy.* Springfield, Ill.: Charles C. Thomas, 1968.

Geyman, J. "Dying and death of a family member." *Journal of Family Practice* 17, no. 1 (1983): 125–34.

Gogan, J.; Koocher, G.; Foster, D.; and O'Malley, J. "Impact of childhood cancer on siblings." *Health and Social Work* 2, no. 1 (1977): 42–57.

Gogan, J.; O'Malley, J.; and Foster, D. "Treating the pediatric cancer patient: A review." *Journal of Pediatric Psychology* 2 (1977): 42–48.

Goldfogel, L. "Working with the parent of a dying child." *American Journal of Nursing* 70, no. 8 (1970): 1675–79.

Greenberg, L.I. "Therapeutic grief work with children." *Social Casework* 56, no. 7 (1975): 396–403. 1975.

Greenham, D., and Lohmann, R. "Children facing death: Recurring patterns of adaptation." *Health and Social Work* 7, no. 2 (1982): 89–94.

Gregory, I. "Anterospective data following childhood loss of a parent." *Archives of General Psychiatry* 13 (1965): 99–120, 110–19.

———. "Retrospective data concerning childhood loss of a parent: I and II." *Archives of General Psychiatry* 15 (1966): 354–67.

Grollman, E.A., ed. *Explaining Death to Children.* Boston: Beacon Press, 1967.

———. *Talking about Death.* Boston: Beacon Press, 1971.

Hagin, R., and Corwin, C. "Bereaved children." *Journal of Clinical Child Psychology* 3, no. 2 (1974): 39–40.

Hajal, F. "Post-suicide grief work in family therapy." *Journal of Marriage and Family Counselling* 3, no. 2 (1977): 35–42.

Hare-Mustin, B. "Family therapy following the death of a child." *Journal of Marital and Family Therapy* 5, no. 2 (1979): 51.

Harrison, S. I.; Davenport, C.W.; and McDermott, J.F. "Children's reactions to bereavement: Adult confusions and misperceptions." *Archives of General Psychiatry* (1967): 593–97.

Herbert, B., Jr. "Significance of maternal bereavement before age of eight in psychiatric patients." *Archives of Neurology and Psychiatry* 62 (1949): 630–37.

Hilgard, J.; Newman, M.; and Fisk, F. "Strength of adult ego following childhood bereavement." *American Journal of Orthopsychiatry* 30 (1960): 788–98.

Hilgard, I. "Depressive and psychotic states as anniversaries to sibling death in childhood." *International Psychiatry Clinics* 6 (1969): 197–211.

Hoelter, J., and Hoelter, J. "On interrelationships among exposure to death and dying, fear of death and anxiety." *OMEGA: Journal of Death and Dying* 11, no. 3 (1980–81): 241–54.

Jackson, E. *Telling a Child About Death.* New York: Channel Press, 1965.

Jaglon, M. "Reactions of three schizophrenic patients to their brother's death." *Annals of Psychiatry and Related Disciplines* 11(1973): 54–65.

Johnson, P., and Rosenblatt, P. "Grief following childhood loss of a parent." *American Journal of Psychotherapy* 35, no. 3 (1981): 419–25.

Kaffman, M., and Elizur, E. "Bereavement responses of kibbutz and non-kibbutz children following the death of the father." *Journal of Child Psychology and Psychiatry and Allied Disciplines* 24, no. 3 (1983): 435–42.

Kalnins, I.V. "The dying child: A new perspective." *Journal of Pediatric Psychology* 2 (1977): 39–41.

Karon, M., and Vernick, J. "An approach to the emotional support of fatally ill children." *Clinical Pediatrics* 7, no. 5 (1968): 274–80.

Kastenbaum, R. "Time and death in adolescence." In *The Meaning of Death*, edited by H . Feifel. New York: McGraw-Hill, 1959.

———. "The child's understanding of death: How does it develop?" In *Explaining Death to Children*, edited by E.A. Grollman. Boston: Beacon Press, 1967.

Kirkley-Best, E., and Kellner, K. "The forgotten grief: A review of the psychology of stillbirth." *American Journal of Orthopsychiatry* 52, no. 3 (1982): 420–29.

Kliman, G. "Facilitation of mourning during childhood." In *Perspectives on Bereavement*, edited by J. Gerber et al. New York: Arno Press, 1979.

Koocher, G.P. "Conversations with children about death—Ethical considerations in research." *Journal of Clinical Child Psychology* 3, no. 2 (1974): 19–21.

———. "Talking with children about death." *American Journal of Orthopsychiatry*, 44, no. 3 (1974): 404–41.

Koocher, G. P.; O'Malley, J.E.; Foster, D.; and Gogan, J.L. "Death anxiety in normal children and adolescents." *Psychiatria Clinica* 9 (1976): 220–29.

Krell, R., and Rabkin, L. "The effects of sibling death on the surviving child: A family perspective." *Family Process* 18, no. 4 (1979): 471–77.

Kubler-Ross, E. *On Death and Dying.* New York: Macmillan, 1969.

———. "The languages of dying." *Journal of Clinical Child Psychology* 3 (1973): 22–24.

———. *On Children and Death.* New York: Macmillan, 1983.

Kung, F. "From diagnosis to survival." In *Living with Childhood Cancer*, edited by J. Spinetta and P. Deasy-Spinetta. St. Louis: C.V. Mosby, 1981.

Lansky, S.; Stephenson, L.; Weller, E.; Cavins, G., Jr.; and Cavins, N. "Failure to thrive during infancy in siblings of pediatric cancer patients." *American Journal of Pediatric Hematology/Oncology,* 4, no. 4 (1982): 361–66.

Lavigne, J., and Ryan, M. "Psychological adjustments of siblings of children with chronic illness." *Pediatrics* 63, no. 4 (1979): 616–27.

Lester, D., and Kam, G. "Effect of a friend dying upon attitudes toward death." *Journal of Social Psychology* 83 (1971): 149–50.

Levinson, B.M. "The pet and the child's bereavement." *Mental Hygiene* 51 (1967): 197–200.

Leviton, D. "The need for education on death and suicide." *Journal of School Health* 39 (1969): 370–74.

Lewis, M., and Lewis, D. "Dying children and their families." In *The Child and Death*, edited by J. Schowalter et al. New York: Columbia University Press, 1983.

Leyn, R. "Terminally ill children and their families: A study of the variety of responses to fatal illness." *Maternal and Child Nursing Journal* 5 (1976): 179–88.

Lindemann, E. "Symptomatology and management of acute grief." *American Journal of Psychiatry* 101 (1944): 141–48.

Lindsay, M., and MacCarthy, D. "Caring for the brothers and sisters of a dying child."

In *Care of the Child Facing Death,* edited by L. Burton. London: Routledge & Kegan Paul, 1974.

Lipton, H. "The dying child and the family: The skills of the social worker." In *The Child and Death,* edited by O.J. Sahler. St. Louis: C.V. Mosby, 1978.

Mahan, C.; Schreiner, R.; and Green, M. "Bibliotherapy: A tool to help parents mourn their infant's death." *Health and Social Work* 8, no. 2 (1983): 126–32.

Mahler, M. "Helping children to accept death." *Child Study* 27 (1950): 98–120.

Markusen, E., and Fulton, R. "Childhood bereavement and behavior disorders: A critical review." *OMEGA: Journal of Death and Dying* 2 (1971): 107–17.

Martin, H.L. et al. "The family of the fatally burned child." *Lancet* 2 (1968): 628–29.

Martinson, I.M., ed. *Home Care for the Dying Child.* New York: Appleton-Century-Crofts, 1976.

———. "Home care for children dying of cancer." *Pediatrics* 62, no. 1 (1978): 106–13.

May, H., and Breme, F. "SIDS family adjustment scale: A method of assessing family adjustment to Sudden Infant Death Syndrome." *OMEGA: Journal of Death and Dying* 13, no. 1 (1982–83): 59–74.

McCollum, A., and Schwartz, A. "Social work and the mourning parent." *Social Work* 17, no. 1 (1972): 25–36.

Miller, J. "Children's reactions to the death of parent: A review of the psychoanalytic literature." *Journal of the American Psychoanalytic Association* 19, no. 4 (1971): 697–719.

Mills, G. et al. *Discussing Death: A Guide to Death Education.* Palm Springs, Calif.: ETC Publications, 1976.

Mitchell, M. *The Child's Attitude to Death.* New York: Schocken Books, 1967.

Mitchell, N., and Schulman, K. "The child and fear of death." In *The Child and Death,* edited by J. Schowalter et al. New York: Columbia University Press, 1983.

Moellenhoff, F. "Ideas of children about death." *Bulletin of the Menninger Clinic* 3 (1939): 148–56.

Moller, H. "Death: Handling the subject and affected students in schools." In *Explaining Death to Children,* edited by E.A. Grollman. Boston: Beacon Press, 1967.

Moriarty, I. "Mourning the death of an infant: The sibling's story." *Journal of Pastoral Care* 32, no. 1 (1918): 22–23.

Morrisey, J. "A note on interviews with children facing death." *Social Casework* 44 (1963): 343–45.

———. "Children's adaptation to fatal illness." *Journal of Social Work* 8, no. 4 (1963): 81–88.

Nagera, H. "Children's reactions to the death of important objects: A developmental approach." *Psychoanalytic Study of the Child* 25 (1970): 360–400.

Nagy, M. "The child's theories concerning death." *Journal of Genetic Psychology* 73, 1st half (1948): 3–27.

———. "The child's view of death." In *The Meaning of Death,* edited by H. Feifel. New York: McGraw-Hill, 1959.

Natterson, J., and Knudson, A. "Observations concerning fear of death in fatally ill children and their mothers." *Psychosomatic Medicine* 22, no. 6 (1960): 456–65.

Northrup, F.C. "Dying child." *American Journal of Nursing* 74, no. 6 (1974): 1066–68.

Orbac, C. "The multiple meanings of the loss of a child." *American Journal of Psychotherapy* 13, no. 4 (1959): 906–15.

Owen, G.; Fulton, R.; and Markusen, E. "Death at a distance: A study of family survivors." *OMEGA: Journal of Death and Dying* 13, no. 3 (1982–83): 191–225.

Palombo, J. "Parent loss and childhood bereavement: Some theoretical considerations." *Clinical Social Work Journal* 9, no. 1 (1981): 3–33.

Parad, H., ed. *Crisis Interevention: Selected Readings.* New York: Family Service Association of America, 1965.

Peretz, D. "Reactions to loss." In *Loss and Grief: Psychological Management in Medical Practice,* edited by B. Shoenberg et al. New York: Columbia University Press, 1970.

Pincus, L. *Death and the Family.* New York: Pantheon Books, 1975.

Pollock, G. "Childhood parent and sibling loss in adult patients." *Archives of General Psychiatry* 7 (1982): 295–305.

———. "On siblings, childhood sibling loss and creativity." *Annual of Psychoanalysis* 6 (1978).

Prichard, E., and Collard, J., eds. *The Family And Death: Social Work Perspectives.* New York: Columbia University Press, 1977.

Rando, T. "An investigation of grief and adaptation in parents whose children have died from cancer." *Journal of Pediatric Psychology* 8, no. 1 (1983): 3–20. 1983.

Rochlin, G. "How younger children view death and themselves." In *Explaining Death to Children,* edited by E.A. Grollman. Boston: Beacon Press, 1967.

Rogers, R., in collaboration with M.N. Weisman, eds. "Children's reaction to sibling death." *Psychosomatic Medicine: Proceedings of the First International Congress of the Academy of Psychosomatic Medicine,* Palma de Malorca, Spain, Sept. 12–16, 1966. Amsterdam, N.Y.: Excerpta Medica Foundation, 1967.

Rosen, H. "Prohibitions against mourning in childhood sibling loss." *OMEGA: Journal of Death and Dying* 15, no. 4 (1984–85): 307–16.

Rosen, H., and Cohen, H. "Children's reactions to sibling loss." *Clinical Social Work Journal* 9, no. 3 (1981): 211–19.

Rosenblatt, B. "A young boy's reaction to the death of his sister." *Journal of the American Academy of Child Psychiatry* 8 (1969): 321–35.

Rosenblatt, P.; Walsh, R.; and Jackson, D. *Grief and Mourning in Cross-cultural Perspective.* HRAF Press, 1976.

Rosenzweig, S. "Sibling death as a psychological experience with special reference to schizophrenia." *Psychoanalytic Review* 30 (1943): 177–86.

Rosenzweig, S., and Bray, D. "Sibling deaths in the anamneses of schizophrenic patients." *Archives of Neurology and Psychiatry* 49 (1943): 71–92.

Ross, E. "Children's books related to death: A discussion." In *Explaining Death to Children,* edited by E.A. Grollman. Boston: Beacon Press, 1967.

Salladay, S., and Royal, M. "Children and death: Guidelines for grief work." *Child Psychiatry & Human Development* 11, no. 4: 203–212.

Sanders, C. "A comparison of adult bereavement in the death of a spouse, child and parent." *OMEGA: Journal of Death and Dying* 10, no. 4 (1979–80): 303–22.

Saunders, C. "The management of fatal illness in childhood." *Proceedings of the Royal Society of Medicine* 62, no. 6 (1969): 550–53.

Schiff, H. *The Bereaved Parent.* New York: Penguin Books, 1977.

Schilder, P., and Weschler, D. "The attitudes of children towards death." *Journal of Genetic Psychology* 45 (1934): 406–51.

Schoenberg, B.; Carr, A.; Peretz, D.; and Kutscher, A. *Loss and Grief: Psychological Management in Medical Practice.* New York: Columbia University Press, 1970.

Schoenberg, B.; Carr, A.; Kutscher, A.; Peretz, D.; and Goldbert, I. *Anticipatory Grief.* New York: Columbia University Press, 1974.

Schoenberg, B.; Gerber, I.; Weiner, A.; Kutscher, A.; Peretz, D.; and Carr, A., eds. *Bereavement: Its Psychosocial Aspects.* New York: Columbia University Press, 1975.

Schowalter, J. E. "Parent death and child bereavement." In *Bereavement: Its Psychosocial Aspects,* edited by Schoenberg, B., Gerber, I., Wiener, A., Kutscher, A., Peretz, D., and Carr, A. New York: Columbia University Press, 1975.

Shambaugh, B. "A study of loss reactions in a 7-year-old." *Psychoanalytic Study of the Child* 16 (1961): 510–23.

Share, L. "Family communication in the crises of a child's fatal illness: A literature review and analysis." *OMEGA: Journal of Death and Dying* 3, no. 30 (1972): 187–201.

Shneidman, E. *Death and the College Student.* New York: Behavioral Theory Publications, 1972.

Smith, A., and Schneider, L. "The dying child: Helping the family cope with impending death." *Clinical Pediatrics* 8 (1969): 131–34.

Solnit, A. "The dying child." *Developmental Medicine and Child Neurology* 7 (1965): 693–95.

———. "Emotional management of family stressed in care of dying child." *Pediatric Currents* 17, no. 8 (1968): 65.

Solnit, A., and Green, M. "The pediatric management of the dying child: Part II. The child's reaction to the fear of dying." In *Modern Perspectives in Child Development.* New York: International Universities Press, 1963.

Sourkes, B. "Siblings of the pediatric cancer patient." In *Psychological Aspects of Childhood Cancer,* edited by J. Kellerman. Springfield, Ill.: Charles C. Thomas, 1981.

Spinetta, J. "The dying child's awareness of death: A review." *Psychological Bulletin* 81 (1974): 256–60.

———. "The sibling of the child with cancer." In *Living with Childhood Cancer,* edited by J. Spinetta and P. Deasy-Spinetta. St. Louis: C.V. Mosby, 1981.

Spinetta, J., and Deasy-Spinetta, P. "Talking with children who have a life-threatening illness." In *Living with Childhood Cancer,* edited by J. Spinetta and P. Deasy-Spinetta. St. Louis: C.V. Mosby, 1981.

Spinetta, J., and Maloney, L. "Death anxiety in the out-patient leukemic child." *Pediatrics* 56 (1975): 1034–37.

———. "The child with cancer: Patterns of communication and denial." *Journal of Consulting and Clinical Psychology* 46 (1978): 1540–41.

Spinetta, J.; Rigler, D.; and Karon, M. "Anxiety in the dying child." *Pediatrics* 52, no. 8 (1973): 841–45.

Tallmer, M.; Formanek, R.; and Tallmer, J. "Factors influencing children's concepts of death." *Journal of Clinical Child Psychology* 3, no. 2 (1974): 17–19.

Teitz, W.; McSherry, L.; and Britt, B. "Family sequelae after a child's death due to cancer." *American Journal of Psychotherapy* 31, no. 3 (1977): 417–25.

Tennant, C.; Bebbington, P.; and Hurry, J. "Parental death in childhood and risk of adult depressive disorders: A review." *Psychological Medicine*, 10, no. 2 (1980): 289–99.

Toch, R. "Management of the child with a fatal disease." *Clinical Pediatrics* 3, no. 7 (1964): 418–27.

Troup, E., ed. *The Patient, Death and the Family.* New York: Scribner, 1974.

Valdes-Dapena, M. "Sudden infant death syndrome: A review of the medical literaure 1974–1979." *Pediatrics* 66, no. 4 (1980): 597–613.

Vernick, J., and Karon, M. "Who's afraid of death on a leukemia ward." *American Journal of Diseases of Children* 109 (1965): 393–97.

Von Hug-Hellmuth, H. "The child's concept of death." *Psychoanalytic Quarterly* 34 (1965): 499–516.

Vore, D.A. "Child's view of death." *Southern Medical Journal* 67, no. 4 (1974): 383–85.

Waechter, E. "Death anxiety in children with fatal illness." Ph.D. diss., Stanford University, 1968.

———. "Children's awareness of fatal illness." *American Journal of Nursing* 71, no. 6 (1971): 1168–72.

Weiner, J. "Reaction of the family to the fatal illness of a child." In *Loss and Grief: Psychological Management in Medical Practice*, edited by Schoenberg, B.; Carr, A.; Peretz, D.; and Kutscher, A. New York: Columbia University Press, 1970.

Weston, D., and Irwin, R. "Preschool child's response to death of infant sibling." *American Journal of Diseases of Children* 106, no. 6 (1963): 564–67.

Williams, H. "On a teaching hospital's responsibility to counsel parents concerning their child's death." *Medical Journal of Australia* 2, no. 16 (1963): 633–45.

Wold, D.A., and Townes, B.D. "The adjustment of siblings to childhood leukemia." *Family Coordinator* 18 (1969): 1955–60.

Wolf, A. *Helping Your Child to Understand Death.* New York: Child Study Association of America, 1973.

Wolfenstein, M. "How is mourning possible?" *Psychoanalytic Study of the Child* 21 (1966): 93–123.

———. "Loss, rage and repetition." *Psychoanalytic Study of the Child* 24 (1969): 432–60.

Wolfenstein, M., and Kliman, G., eds. *Children and the Death of a President.* Garden City: Doubleday, 1965.

Wright, L. "Emotional support for parents of dying children." *Journal of Clinical Child Psychology* 3, no. 2 (1974): 37–38.

York, J., and Weinstein, S. "The effect of a videotape about death on bereaved children in family therapy." *OMEGA: Journal of Death and Dying* 11, no. 4 (1980–81): 355–61.

Yudkin, S. "Children and death." *Lancet* 1 (1967): 37–41.

Zeligs, R. "Death casts its shadow on a child." *Mental Hygiene* 51, no. 1 (1967): 9–20.

————. "Children's attitudes towards death." *Mental Hygiene* 51, no. 3 (1967): 393–96.

————, ed. *Children's Experience with Death.* Springfield, Ill.: Charles C. Thomas, 1974.

Zilboorg, G. "Fear of death." *Psychoanalytic Quarterly* 12 (1943): 465–75.

Index

About the Author

Helen Rosen received the M.S.W. degree from New York University and the Ph.D. from Rutgers–The State University of New Jersey. Dr. Rosen is currently assistant professor in social work at Rutgers in Camden, New Jersey. She has published articles in several professional journals on child abuse, hospitalized children, and childhood sibling loss.